Wicca Spells

Discover The Power of Wiccan Spells, Herbal Magic, Essential Oils & Witchcraft Rituals For Wiccans, Witches & Other Practitioners of Magic

Sofia Visconti

© **Copyright 2020 Sofia Visconti - All rights reserved.**

The content contained within this book may not be reproduced, duplicated, or transmitted without direct written permission from the author or the publisher.

Under no circumstances will any blame or legal responsibility be held against the publisher, or author, for any damages, reparation, or monetary loss due to the information contained within this book, either directly or indirectly.

Legal Notice:

This book is copyright protected. It is only for personal use. You cannot amend, distribute, sell, use, quote or paraphrase any part, or the content within this book, without the consent of the author or publisher.

Disclaimer Notice:

Please note the information contained within this document is for educational and entertainment purposes only. All effort has been executed to present accurate, up to date, reliable, complete information. No warranties of any kind are declared or implied. Readers acknowledge that the author is not engaging in the rendering of legal, financial, medical, or professional advice. The content within this book has been derived from various sources. Please consult a licensed professional before attempting any techniques outlined in this book.

By reading this document, the reader agrees that under no circumstances is the author responsible for any losses, direct or indirect, that are incurred as a result of the use of the information contained within this document, including, but not limited to, errors, omissions, or inaccuracies.

Introduction

Wicca is mostly practiced in the West and has its roots in the occult. It is a modern movement based on pagan beliefs and practices common in Northern and Western Europe before Christianity became the religion people followed. It is mostly girls, and women follow Wicca since the focus of the religion is on goddess worship and female power. Wicca comes from the word wicce, which means "to bend or shape nature to your service," and this is the basis of this practice. Wiccans cast spells or perform rituals only when their intent is to make changes in the physical world. They often use spells for protection, healing, fertility and to banish negative influences.

Most people are unaware of this religion, and some have developed a fear of it because they are unaware of what it actually is or have been told false or misleading information about it.

There are some who are brave enough to follow this religion, and research shows that there are over 10,000 witches in the country. Research shows that many people now choose to follow Wicca, Pagan and neo-Pagan religions. According to the Pagan Federation, there are over 100,000 people who follow various Pagan rituals and practices.

I have explained the various aspects of Wicca, and its practices and beliefs in my best-selling book, 'Wicca for Beginners: Discover The World of Wicca, Magic, Wiccan Beliefs, Rituals & Witchcraft.' Many readers have requested additional content on spells and magic, so in this book,

"*Wicca Spells: Discover The Power of Wiccan Spells, Herbal Magic, Essential Oils & Witchcraft Rituals. For Wiccans, Witches & Other Practitioners of Magic*' I will delve deeper into the realms of wiccan magic.

Wiccan Practices and Beliefs

Wicca is a practice that recognizes two divinities – the Horned God or God and the Goddess, which means it is a theistic practice. In traditional Wicca practices, God is the primary deity. In the feminist or modern approach of Wicca, the goddess is the primary deity. Some groups also recognize the goddess as the only deity. The guard is associated with forests and sun while the goddess is associated with the sea, stars, and moon. The latter is also known as the mother goddess. The followers of this movement focused on one or both deities and the elements of nature during their worship. The practices of divination, incantations, and witchcraft are some significant practices of Wicca.

Some detailed and specific Wiccan beliefs are slightly hard to identify since there is no authoritative or singular book that any Wiccan lives by. Many different groups use this religion or practice. Wicca does not adhere to any specific truth or doctrine but focuses more on how the individual practices the religion in the form of rituals, witchcraft, ceremonies, etc. Having said that, most followers of this practice adhere to some basic practices and beliefs.

- Every Wiccan observes annual holidays or Sabbats with ceremonies and rituals.

- They respect and worship all the elements – air, water, fire and earth, and spirit, which is the first element. According to Wicca, the spirit is present in every element.

- Wiccans do not believe that magic is supernatural. They believe that magic is the intentional manipulation of the various elements.

- Another common Wiccan belief is that they should not harm themselves or others.

- Wiccans also do their best to uphold the Threefold Law, and this law is based on karma. During any ritual, a witch may emit some magic or energy, and according to the Threefold Law, this energy returns to the witch three times.

- Since the Wiccan religion is open, it does not believe in evangelizing people. This practice accepts other religions and borrows some rituals and practices from them.

- According to the Wiccan religion, people are either reborn or reincarnated after death.

Occult and Wicca

Modern Wicca is influenced by Aleister Crowley, Doreen Valiente, and Gerald Gardner. This is rooted in the occult, referring to various matters that involve the action or influence of various supernormal and supernatural phenomena or powers.

Wicca and the Bible

Worship the Lord Alone

Wiccans always honor the Wiccan deities and the natural elements. The Bible, however, teaches people that they must worship only God and not his creation, according to Exodus 20:3, Psalm 104, and Luke 4:8. Wiccans, however, believe in creation worship, and this is not new. The Apostle Paul was disappointed with this behavior, and he lamented in Roman 1:25, and said, "They exchanged the truth about God for a lie, and worshiped and served created things rather than the Creator—who is forever praised. Amen."

The Lord is Sovereign

Wiccans rely only on the power they find in themselves, other spiritual forces of nature. The Bible, however, forbids this. According to Deuteronomy 18:9-13 and Leviticus 19:31, this act is not only forbidden but is also futile since the Lord possesses complete power and control over everything in the universe. This means that an outcome accomplished through a spell or ritual is often a trick designed to deceive any person and deviate his focus from God. This deceiver will be thrown into an eternal lake of fire, and must never be sought after or followed.

The Lord is the Truth

People who practice Wicca are always asked to do whatever they want, as long as they do not harm any individual. Their actions must never cause harm to anybody, including themselves. This rule is, however, impossible to keep since nobody knows the full effect of their actions. The Wiccan Rede says that practitioners can do what they want, but harm is a relative concept.

Now that you have a basic idea about what Wicca is, let us dive into the world of witchcraft and magic. This book has all the information you need to know about Wicca and teaches you the basic rules you must adhere to. It helps you learn more about how to protect yourself and the people around you when you cast a spell. You'll also learn a few spells you can use to improve your physical and mental wellbeing, attract love and friendship, and protect yourself and your home.

All the information in the book is explained in simple terms, and the spells explained in the book are broken down into step-by-step instructions. So, if you want to change your life for the better without causing harm to anybody else, then consider a Wiccan spell to help you make that change. Regardless of whether you are a beginner or a Wiccan looking for new spells to add to your book of shadows, you do not have to look any further. This book has everything you need to satiate your desires.

Chapter One: Getting Started
What to Consider When Casting Spells
Always Use the Wiccan Rede

According to the Wiccan Rede, you can do anything you want as long as your actions do not cause any harm to people around you. People interpret this statement in different ways. They may also ask the following questions:

1. What does it mean to harm someone?

2. Who should we not harm?

The bottom line is that spell casters must always take personal responsibility for their actions. If you are unsure of what your actions will amount to, make sure to keep your intentions simple and clear.

Never Cast Spells to Manipulate Others

This comes from the point above, and it tells us there may be times when we may want to change the way someone behaves. When we do this, we may cause harm to them. Never use your spells to change how someone thinks, behaves, or acts. You shouldn't do anything to influence their decisions. If you deal with someone who abuses or harasses you, and if the person is toxic, then you should do your best to help them understand the consequences of their actions. You can also wish for you or them to find realization and success away from each other. It is always best to seek justice and not revenge. Always let the universe provide them their punishment.

Do Not Cast Spells on Behalf of Others

It is always good to use your powers to help people around you, but you must do it responsibly. If you do want to cast spells on behalf of others, ensure that you obtain their permission before you do that. Never impose your practices and beliefs on people around you. Give the person enough space, so they come to you and ask for help. Do not attempt any spiritual work on people without their permission.

Keep Your Work Private

There is some meaning behind the superstition, "If you tell people what you wished for, it will not come true." Witches could never talk about their powers or spirituality openly for many years since they were afraid of being punished or persecuted. People now talk freely about their beliefs and practices, but people need to respect others. They must never boast about their spiritual practices, especially when nobody has asked about them. Let us understand why you should not do this. When you tell someone about what you want to do, their feelings about the practice may interfere directly or indirectly with your practice. You need to ensure that you always perform your magic in safe or private places. Within a circle or coven of trust, people can share their energy if they work towards the same intentions or goals.

Protect the Environment and Nature

Always use biodegradable tools and materials whenever you perform any spells. This helps you reduce your carbon footprint. When you clean after yourself, disposing of everything you use for your ritual, ensure you are conscious about how you do this. Make sure to always clean up after yourself when you perform magic in nature. The best thing to do is always to purchase ethically sourced or fair trade ingredients. It is best to purchase these ingredients locally or try making tinctures or grow your herbs at home.

Be Safe

If you want to use candles when you cast spells, make sure they are placed in sturdy holders. Do not place them close to a window with curtains or blinds to avoid fire hazards. Never leave lit candles unattended. If the candle needs to be left burning throughout the night, enclose it in a container or place it on a heatproof dish.

Stay Protected and Cleanse Yourself

If you feel any energy blockages or disturbances when you perform spells, you must regain your spiritual balance. To do this, think about using bath spells or spiritual cleansing. When you cleanse your body and personal spaces, such as your home or workplace, you can protect yourself from any negative energies or psychic attacks. You can prevent these regular interactions.

Look After Yourself

Healthy minds and healthy bodies go together. If you experiment with essential oils, infusions, potions, or similar, make sure you are careful. Remember that magical practices are not meant to be used in place of proper medical attention. If you think you have a health issue, you must speak to a physician or healthcare provider. Do not leave it to the universe to take care of your problems.

Pre-Ritual Protection

One of the best ways to remove the energy that exists in your space is by using a basic ritual. You can also protect yourself when you cast spells by creating a protective circle. This circle helps to create a space where you can work with high energy. You can increase the strength of the spells you cast based on your intent. Most people create a protective circle before they invoke external forces, energy, or spirits. As a newbie to this, there's no need for you to cast that circle for every ritual. You only need to do this when you need additional protection, control, and focus. Always cast a circle, in particular, when you are going to be working with forces beyond your control. You can channel the energy and enhance it using your circle.

Protective Circle

Protective circles come in all sizes and shapes. Some witches or spell casters cast a sphere, while others look at it only as a circle. Some also choose to cast a triangle, star, or square within the circle. It is best to cast the circle before you begin your ritual since this helps to put you in the right frame of mind. How your spells are cast depends on the following:

- Experience
- Personal beliefs
- Personal preference

Expert practitioners only need to visualize the circle.

Steps to Cast the Wiccan Protective Circle

Determine How Much Space You Need to Perform the Ritual

Cast a big enough circle that you can comfortably move about in when you perform the ritual or cast the spell. If you need to cast the circle, so only you perform the ritual or cast the spell, ensure the circle is big enough to allow you to stretch your arms and legs as far as you can. If you want to move or stand in the circle while you perform the ritual, you must create a larger circle. You should visualize this area using the right stones, rope, candles, chalk, or sand, to demarcate the circle.

Cleaning Your Spell-Casting Area

Your spell-casting or ritual circle must be tidy as it is a symbol of integrity and purity. The circle ensures your safety, so use a vacuum or broom to sweep the area free of debris or dirt. To make certain that the area is clean, remove all negativity by purifying it. You can do this in a few ways; spread salt or saltwater around the area, use incense, use a ritual broom to sweep it, play an instrument of some kind, or use a white sage smudge stick.

Preparing Your Tools and the Altar

Once your area is clean, it's time to prepare your tools and get your altar ready. It doesn't matter what you use as your altar; any surface will do, even a table. You don't even need to buy anything special. If you want, you can cover the floor in front of the altar with a cloth; if it works for you, go for it. Make sure that your altar and the cloth, if you use one, is placed centrally in the circle.

When your altar is placed, you must keep in mind that the objects and materials you use are representative of the directions and the elements, so think carefully when you choose what to use. However you set it up, the cardinal points must be clear; you don't want any confusion when you are performing your ritual or casting spells.

Drawing Your Protective Circle

When you draw your circle around the altar, you can use an Athame, a wand, or your fingers. Whatever you use to draw the circle does not need to touch any surface; you can draw it in the air, if you want, as long as it is a full circle.

Before you begin, stand, close your eyes, and inhale deeply. Relax your body and mind, visualize the energy building up in your body to protect you, increasing with each breath you take. Direct that energy into your dominant hand and arm. Focus on the tool you are going to use to draw your circle; visualize the energy going into it from your hand. See the energy leaving the tool and laying in a protective circle.

You don't have to draw the circle just once; some prefer to draw it a few times. You may, for example, want to draw a circle to protect you, draw it again to provide concentration and again for energy. You can draw as many circles as you need, depending on what you need, or you can draw one circle that encompasses everything. You must always visualize your circle and how to keeps you safe from negativity.

Invoking the Elements

Some witches require the elements and cardinal directions to cast spells, and some rituals also require the spirits and the Divine presence to be invoked. Consider this when you are casting your circle; the elements should be set as follows:

- The air element is invoked in the East. Light incense and place it so it faces East.

- The water element is invoked in the West. Fill a glass with water and place it facing West.

- The fire element is invoked in the South. Place a white candle facing South. White candles are symbolic of the fire element and also provide extra protection.

- The earth element is invoked in the North. Place a bowl of salt facing North.

When you have placed your symbols accordingly, stand in the circle and raise your arms, Close your eyes and say, "I ask God and the Goddess to bless the circle. Within it, I am free and protected. So be it."

Or you can say, "I conceive this circle as a place of contemplation and protection. A space between worlds and time outside time. Bless you."

Once you have spoken the words, your circle is ready for you to perform your ritual or cast your spell.

Opening the Circle to Complete the Ritual

Once your spell is cast, you must complete your ritual by opening the circle, using your wand or Athame. Holding it in your hand, move the wand or Athame in the direction opposite to the one you cast the circle with, this will open the circle. At the same time, say, "I am opening this circle, but I am not breaking it." Or you could say, "I undo this circle; I want to leave this place as it was before the spell was cast."

At all times, show due respect to the nature spirits or the deities summoned when your spell was cast. Always thank them for ensuring the success of your spell, show them honor for helping you. Lastly, extinguish the candles and step out of your circle.

A Few More Tips

• Your protective circle is a sphere of energy. It is powerful, but that power depends on how strongly you visualize it. Keep yourself calm and relaxed by using visualization techniques; the calmer you are, the stronger your focus will be.

• Make sure that you have all your tools and elemental symbols before you begin. The last thing you want is to leave your circle because you forgot an ingredient.

- When it comes time to close the circle, make sure nothing enters or leaves the circle. If you need to interrupt a spell, you must visualize a door or window in your circle. When you enter or leave the circle, do so by this opening and always close it after. Make sure the opening is always facing in the correct direction; that way, when you go through it, you are not interrupting your circle.

Understanding Your Circle

The protective circle you cast is a kind of barrier, keeping you safe from the influence that comes from outside it. Negative energy can get in the way of your concentration, breaking your focus, and this is why many people choose to draw a circle to meditate in; it leaves them free to focus fully on their intent.

If you are practicing at home and a door or a window is opened, your circle will stop the energy disappearing through the opening, and it stops energy from another person interfering with your rituals and spell-casting.

If this is your first time casting a spell, it is natural to feel some anxiety. Your circle is a protective bubble around you, keeping you safe. Inside this circle, you can experiment with casting different spells, and nobody else will be affected. If you want to break your circle, walk carefully across the line, and dismiss the circle. This is important and should never be omitted from your rituals.

Summing Up

Many people opt to use witchcraft, spells, and magic when they want something specific. It could be providing protection for them or their loved ones, attracting good health, money, even the job of their dreams. The spells you cast are classed as "white" magic and are positive. They are designed to help you bring about improvements in life, but they can only work if you carefully follow the guidelines.

Never be scared of trying something, keep your focus on your intent, and ensure your ritual area, your body, and your mind are always clean.

Protective circles are drawn so you can perform meditation, witchcraft, and rituals. Make sure you are familiar with your rituals and spells; never try to do one blind, as it were. Always choose the correct words that will ensure your intent is clear to the universe.

The magic circle has two primary functions:

1. It provides protection for you and anyone around you from negative energies;

2. The energy you channel is held safe within the circle.

Your energy must be contained within the circle until you have finished the ritual. To end the spell, always open your circle to release the energy.

Every witch works differently, and not all witches use protective circles. You must do what is comfortable and right for you.

Secrets to Successful Spell-Casting

Confidence in spell-casting comes with practice and experience, and you won't always be in the right mindset to cast a spell, either. When your mindset or your thoughts change negatively, stop. Do not cast any spells or perform any rituals as there is the potential for them to go wrong or not work at all. The following tips can help you be successful:

Secret #1: Don't Worry That Might Not Work

I realize that may not always be possible, but it's a fact that the more you worry about something going wrong, the more likely it is to go wrong. You may be worried about what would happen if the spell went wrong, or if it would even work. Stop, because this is not putting you in the right frame of mind. Learn to see magic as a way of applying intent and energy. Too much time spent worrying about the spell-casting can lead to negative energy getting in the way of your intent.

Let's say, for example, that your spell is all about finding a decent job. It may take you half an hour to focus your energy and your intent on the spell but willpower will add to the power, making it incredibly powerful. That's all well and good, but if then spend the next few days worrying incessantly over whether the spell will work, all you are doing is directing your energy toward the worry, taking it away from your intent – that spells failure.

The solution is quite simple – stop worrying. Have some faith in yourself and your spells and magic. If you are not in a place where you can trust your spells or magic, you cannot get to where you want to. Always remind yourself that your worry is counterproductive. If you catch yourself worrying about the outcome of a spell, tell yourself to stop. The magic works, and you should avoid disturbing it. Let the magic do its job.

Secret #2: Don't Stress About Details

Did you ever find yourself in a situation where you realized that you were out of olive oil and had to substitute almond oil or stumbled over an incantation? There is so much to learn about spell casting that you might find yourself somewhat overwhelmed. Do not worry; take things slowly and remember that magic is about your intentions, and every step, action, or tool involved when you cast a spell is the best way to channel your energy and solidify your intention.

Almond oil may not align with your intentions as olive oil would, but when you pour enough energy and focus on the oil, you can get the job done. It is tricky to substitute herbs or oils in complex spells, and you may not learn what works for you until you tinker with it. So, do not worry. Always try different substitutions and see how the spell works. If you do not like the results, you can change the elements that do not work for you.

In the same way, forgetting what you were supposed to say or stumbling over a few words in a spell or incantation is not the end of the world. Some witches and spell casters have a stutter, and they can still cast spells. There are times when you will struggle to make it through an incantation. Do not let this frustrate you and ruin the spell.

You need to accept that mishaps happen, and they do not affect the spell that much. You have to understand that every incantation is only about intent. If you are focused on your energy and intent the entire time, the spell will work even if you say a string of nonsense. Always give yourself a break when it comes to small details. You can strive to be perfect when you cast a spell, but do not let imperfect casting make you feel you cannot get it right.

Secret #3: Give Yourself Time to Get into your "Witch Mode"

It takes most people a lot of time to switch from one mode to another. For instance, some may find it difficult to switch from the work mode to time-off mode, and from the usual mode to the witch mode. It is difficult to make this transition, especially if you lead a busy life, and it is recommended that you do not override these transition periods. When we try to skip from one activity to another, we often deny ourselves the necessary space to switch into our witch mode.

The skills you use at work or school are not the skills you can use to cast spells or perform any other activity. People believe they can behave like computers, but what they forget is they are not built that way. Our minds need some time to switch from one task to the next, to change between different skills to your spiritual skills. You need to give yourself enough time, so you can make the transition before you cast the spell.

If you cannot make this transition easily or are impatient, you must create a ritual to ease the process. You can try to perform some activities before you cast a spell, and perform these activities any time you want to cast spells. You can make this process simple or elaborate, depending on your needs. You can take a bath or meditate for a few minutes before you cast a spell. Regardless of what your ritual entails, you need to ensure it is the same ritual you follow before you cast a spell. Your mind builds a connection between spell casting and the ritual, and you can make the transition faster and easier in the long run. It does take some time to implement this ritual, so always give yourself enough space and time so that you can get into the right frame of mind.

Secret #4: Remember to be Theatrical

Since spell work is a personal endeavor for most people, most standard methods are often flat. One of the best ways to move past this is to use psychodrama. This process is where you fake the spell using theatrics. You can dress up, put on some music, create an ambiance that looks witchy, and get into character. You can then perform any spell of your choice. It is always about setting the stage so that you can get into the right mindset. You must create an environment where you feel witchy.

This may feel fake and dramatic initially, but over time, you learn to use these theatrics to cast spells and notice you can produce the necessary results even with these methods. These theatrics help you find the magic within yourself and use it when you cast spells. This is a key factor for most people and helps them silence any doubts they have about their powers.

When you are in character and in a witchy environment, you soon lose yourself in the process. You find that you obtain the necessary results, and the results are better than when you use regular methods. Do not be under the misconception that you must stick to conventional methods or ideas. Always do what you think makes you feel witchy. Use methods or elements that help to set the right mood.

Chapter Two: Practices

If you are a beginner, there are some aspects you must bear a few practices and points in mind.

Ritual Practices

If you are a beginner, always start off small. Try to incorporate some of the rituals mentioned in this section into your routine. This helps you develop a ritual or practice the works best for you. You need to ensure that you develop a routine you want to stick to.

Light a Candle

Most witches and spellcasters say that lighting a candle helps to both calm and center their energy. Try to light a candle when you wake up in the morning while you do your makeup, on your desk at school or work, or even before you go to bed. A sense of calm spreads through your mind and helps to relax you.

Hold a Crystal

One way to connect with various magical tools is to hold them in your palms and focus on their energy. When you want to purchase a crystal, hold it in your palms for a few minutes and focus on the energy in the crystal. You can also meditate to connect with the energy in the crystal. Once you select your crystal, place it under your pillow.

Stir Your Coffee or Tea Counter-Clockwise

If you drink coffee or tea every morning, stir in the counter-clockwise direction using a spoon. This helps to remove any negativity from your day.

Perform Surya Namaskar

Surya Namaskar or sun salutation is a yoga practice that you can perform anywhere. To do this, follow the steps given below:

- Take a deep breath and exhale while you join your palms at the heart center

- Take another deep breath and raise your hands above your head

- Exhale and slowly bend forward. Make sure to keep your knees straight and try to touch your toes. If you are flexible, you can also move your forehead closer to the knees

- Take another breath and shift your hands so your fingers touch the floor in front of your toes. Lift your head up and look forward

- Exhale and bend your head towards your knees

- Take another deep breath and slowly raise your body and lift your arms above your head

- Exhale and bring your hands to your heart's center.

You can perform this sequence as often as you want at home, in whatever room of the house you feel comfortable in

Use Essential Oil Rollers

If you love essential oils, you can carry a glass bottle filled with the oil of your choice. Make sure the bottle has a rollerball. This is a handy piece of equipment to keep in your purse or at your desk. When you need to focus or require a pick-me-up, apply a little oil behind your ears and on your wrists. Inhale the aroma of the oil.

Drink a Cup of Tea

The drinking team is a powerful ritual to keep yourself calm and be mindful. When you choose the herbs or blend for tea, heat the water and watch the tea brew, inhale the aroma and focus only on your breath to calm your mind.

Develop a Skincare Ritual

When you apply moisturizer or sunscreen on your skin, take a moment for yourself and be mindful and quiet. Always pay attention to the process and find a way to calm your thoughts while you apply moisturizer.

Draw Temporary Signs or Sigils

If you love working with runes, symbols, and sigils, draw them for luck or protection in temporary ways. You can draw them on the mirror using face cream, using a spoon while you cook or in your tea or coffee.

Read About Your Day

Find a book or application that tracks all the astrological information about your sun sign. Spend some time every morning to read the predictions, and you do not have to do this for more than five minutes. Just read what kind of energy you may experience during the day.

Focus on the Seasons

You must always be aware of the seasons and their passing. The Wheel of the Year is a huge part of a Witch's path, and we will look into that a little later in this chapter. When you go for a walk or look out the window, you become more mindful of the changes in the seasons.

Sex Magic

Most people are under the impression that sex magic is a kinky term. Some people may relate sex magic to an image of a woman standing naked in front of a fire or cauldron and calling to the universe to bring back her love or to help her find love. Skye Alexander, the author of 'The Modern Guide to Witchcraft,' said this is not what sex magic is. She mentioned that sex magic is not about enhancing or improving one's sex life, but it is something else entirely.

What is Sex Magic?

As mentioned earlier, magic is all about intention. If you want to cast a spell, all you must do is think positively about the spell and be mindful of what you want. The only difference between magic and sex magic is that in the latter, you use sex to practice mindfulness. Through sex magic, you can increase your dynamic sexual energy and creativity and use that to fuel your spells and intentions. The essence of sex magic is to harness your sexual experiences and the emotions you feel during the experience, including the expectation, tension, pleasure, and happiness that comes with having sex, to focus only on your intentions and desires. You can think about sex magic in the following way – when you blow out your candles on your birthday, you are excited to make a wish. Instead of using excitement to make the wish, you use the pleasure of sex to let the Universe know your intentions. This is sex magic.

Western culture has adopted the use of magic in different areas and aspects of life. The magic used in this culture is intended to attract something or create some kind of outcome in the spell caster's life. Sex magic is quite popular among witches now, but it does have ancient roots. Historical texts and excerpts show that sex magic and sexual practices were quite common in the earlier days, and these practices were accepted and widespread than they are today. Rome and Greece have evidence of sex magic, and there is some proof that people in India and China also used to practice sex magic. Since both sex and magic became a taboo, people never practiced it openly. When people used sex magic, they were happy and were able to stay mindful and positive about what they want in life.

How to Perform Sex Magic?

You must focus quite a bit if you want to use your orgasm as a source of energy for magic. The most important thing to remember is to never rush to the finish line. Try to lengthen the process and see what happens during the entire experience. Understand your emotions and feelings. Skye recommends that people should slow their experience down when they have sex and reach the brink of an orgasm at least three times before they allow themselves to come. People need to enjoy the experience fully and move towards the finish line but stop themselves when they near the end of the line and push back. They should relax and repeat the process again.

Before you have sex, you must set the goal or intention. Ask yourself whether you want to attract money, success at work, heal from heartbreak, attract love, or prevent something from happening in your life. You need to bear this goal in mind during the process. Let us assume you want to attract money, so you must hold this intention in mind when you have sex. After you bring yourself to the brink of an orgasm thrice, finally let go with the intention clear in your mind. Release the energy with the thought in mind and allow yourself to come. You send the intention out into the universe using the same energy to project and release the thought. Once you reach an orgasm, stop thinking or worrying about the intention and let it go.

This gives rise to the question – "How do I think about attracting money when I am about to orgasm?" There are ways to help you focus and make it easier for you to enhance the experience. Many people find it easier to draw images and stick those images within their sights. They can use either tape these images to the ceiling or wall and can look at them before they come. This way, they only focus on the image and intent when they come and do not think about anything else. Some also choose to draw pictures of the intent on their partner's body when they have sex. Others use aromatics, such as lavender oil, frankincense, lemon, and peppermint, to help them concentrate.

Whom Can You Perform Sex Magic With?

It is absolutely fine if you do not have a partner. You do not always need a partner to perform sex magic. You can harness the power and intensity of your sexuality without someone else. You can also do sex magic with those people who are not committed to you as your partner. You can also perform this type of magic with someone you do not love. Skye recommends that you always choose a partner whom you respect. You also need to make your intentions clear when you have sex with the person. There is a lot of respect and trust involved for your partner during the process. You are using this experience to manifest an intention or thought that matters to you. When your mind is clear and more focused on your intentions, you can manifest your thoughts more easily. So, it is best to let your partner know what you want to do, so the process works for you.

Always set the intention together. You should discuss your intentions and thoughts with your partner and let them know what you want to achieve. This way, you both work towards the same goal, and otherwise, you may end up doing different things or wanting different things during the process. The goal of sex magic becomes blurry, and this makes it hard to manifest your intention. Always enter the experience respectfully so that you can manifest your intention positively. It is also okay if the process does not work for you. When you go through the process of sex magic, you end up having some amazing sex regardless of whether you could manifest your intentions in the universe. When you choose a partner you trust, communicate your needs, and make the experience long, sensual, and slow, you are in for a great experience. So, why not try it?

Wheel of the Year

The Wiccan practice is quite flexible, but there is one important element that every Wiccan must follow – the Wheel of the Year, the structural center of the Wiccan practice, or religion. There are eight holidays in the Wiccan year, known as the Sabbats, and these provide Wiccans with occasions to come together with other Wiccans, whether it is to have an informal celebration or to perform coven rituals.

Since Wiccans are solitary practitioners, they know they join their energy with the energy of millions of other practitioners across the globe when they perform their Sabbat rituals.

The Sabbats

The Sabbats are known as the days of the sun and earth. The Sabbats are comprised of four Earth festivals and four solar holidays, namely:

1. Earth Festivals occurring in February, May, August, and October

2. Two solstices

3. Two equinoxes

The first set of holidays or Sabbats are the days when the solar points in the calendar cross each other. For example, Wiccans celebrate Beltane on May 1, and this Sabbat falls between the Summer Solstice and Spring Equinox.

There are four holidays, namely Imbolc, Beltane, Lammas, and Samhain, that fall on days when the quarters cross. These are inspired by traditional or folk festivals that were celebrated before people adopted Christianity in Western Europe. The names of these festivals go by different names depending on the type or form of Wicca that people want to follow. Wiccans who follow Celtic traditions call Lammas as Lughnasa.

Some Wiccan traditions refer to Earth days as Greater Sabbats and cross-quarter or solar holidays as Lesser Sabbats since the former days are filled with great energy. They do this only to help Wiccans differentiate between the types of Sabbats, but it does not mean the solar days are not as important.

How did the Wheel Come into Existence?

It is important to note that Wiccans are not the only ones who follow the eight holidays since numerous Pagan traditions also follow these holidays. Some of these traditions may observe all or only some of the Sabbats. The Wiccan version of the Sabbats is unique since there is a metaphorical myth surrounding the Goddess and God. According to Wiccan texts, God and Goddess are responsible for creating nature. Each of these deities plays a divine and crucial role in the yearly cycles of animal and plant life.

According to Wiccans, God and Goddess represent the Sun and Earth, respectively, and one can view the relationship between the two in the following ways:

1. Mother and child

2. Procreating lovers

Wiccans use the absence and presence of sunlight and warmth across different seasons to understand the Wheel. The story goes as follows: God is born and grows up. Once he reaches his height of power, he does great things before he begins to age. When he nears his end, he fades away and dies before he is reborn as another being. The cycle continues every year. The Goddess is the Earth and is both the mother and creative partner to God. She is always present even when there is no light and warmth. Since the Earth is a constant in the cycle, any festival that symbolizes or worships the Earth is said to have greater power. This cycle depicts the balance between the male and female energies in the Universe, and every Sabbat is used to represent the particular stage in the life cycle.

The High Points in the Calendar

What do you think happens during a Sabbat ritual? The details of the celebration can vary, like every other element in Wicca. Generally speaking, the ritual focuses on some elements that represent the relationship shared by the two deities, and the Sabbat itself. For example, Summer and Spring Sabbats always take the theme of abundance and fertility, while the Autumn Sabbats are associated with reproduction or harvesting.

Most Wiccans always complete the Sabbat ritual, followed by a feast. These proceedings can either be elaborate or simple, and some of these rituals may involve only one practitioner, an informal Wiccan gathering, coven, or circle. Some circles and covens also hold their rituals publicly, so other members may always come and join them. People do not have to be a part of the celebration. Others may choose to perform this celebration in secrecy or celebrate in private.

The details about the ritual, including the food and decorations, are dependent on the Sabbat. Some witches may choose to devote specific parts of their rituals to some aspects of the deities at various times or points during the Wheel of the Year. They may also leave some appropriate offerings on every season and also decorate or add some objects to the altar to create seasonal themes. Some of the common names for each Sabbat used on the Calendar are listed below. The dates when these Sabbats are observed also are mentioned below:

Sabbat	Date
Yule / Winter Solstice	December 20-23*
Imbolc	February 1-2*
Ostara / Spring Equinox	March 19-21*
Beltane	April 30-May 1*
Litha / Summer Solstice	June 20-22*
Lammas	August 1-2*
Mabon / Autumn Equinox	September 21-24*
Samhain	October 31-NOVEMBER 1*

Both the solstices and equinoxes may fall on different dates in some parts of the world since these events occur at specific moments. Thus the day they fall on may also vary from one year to the next, and therefore, there are numerous dates for when people can maintain the Solar holidays or Sabbats.

You must practice the wheel of the year if you want to understand it fully. You should celebrate every Sabbat even if you only do something simple. After a few weeks or months, you get the hang of it, and soon you can attune your thoughts to the energy of every Sabbat. You must bear in mind that any Wiccan practice is not limited only to the Wheel of the Year since Wiccans also celebrate 13 lunar cycles every year when they perform the Esbat rituals.

The Extended Wheel of the Year

It is easy to customize the wheel for yourself by adding extra holidays that speak to your energy. Some examples are given below:

Valentine's Day/Lupercalia

This holiday is observed on February 14. Lupercalia is a Roman ancestor, and Valentine's Day is celebrated in his honor. You can celebrate this holiday by performing a ritual even though this is not an official Sabbat. You can make this a day where you celebrate love in all forms. The ritual must go beyond roses and chocolate, and you can maybe practice sex magic.

Birthday

Your birthday is special for you. Since you do not share your birthday with anybody, you know, unless you are a twin, it is your day of power. This day is the perfect time to celebrate yourself and connect with your inner or higher self.

Earth Day

Since Wiccans have a special connection to the earth, on Earth Day, you must spend some time to take care of the environment around you. For example, you can cast a spell to heal the environment around you.

Fathers' Day and Mothers' Day

Since the family is important for most people, you can integrate these days into your personal Wheel of the Year. You can celebrate fatherhood and motherhood and hold rituals to help you celebrate your loved ones.

The Bottom-Line

The Wheel of the Year may seem extremely simple, but when you dig deeper, you learn there is more to the wheel. It is not only a simple calendar. As mentioned earlier, you must practice this wheel if you want to understand it. With time, you learn to find your meaning with the different Sabbats. If you are new to this religion, it may be difficult to follow the wheel since the rituals may overwhelm you. Instead, celebrate the wheel only by performing simple rituals. When you understand each Sabbat, it becomes natural to you, and it becomes easier for you to follow the Wheel of the Year. Regardless of where you are in your journey, you must remember to know which Sabbat you want to celebrate and why.

Rites of Passage

This section sheds some light on the different rites of passage every Wiccan follower goes through.

Initiation

When someone begins to study the craft or joins a coven, they must complete their initiation ritual. When they do this, British Traditional Wiccans can always trace their lineage during the initiation ritual back to Gerald Gardner. They can then trace their lineage back from Gerald to the New Forest coven. Gardner also believed there is a traditional length to every year. When people begin to study the craft, they should go through an initiation ceremony. However, Gardner did break the rules quite often when he practiced the craft.

In Britain, traditional Wicca practices only accept someone into the first degree of Wicca. If they want to proceed to the second degree, they must go through a ceremony where they must name and describe every tool they use during rituals, and how they implement these tools. The practitioners are given their craft names during this ritual, and when they hold the second degree, they can initiate others into the craft. They can also start their own covens, but these are only semi-autonomous.

The third degree is the highest honor in British Wicca, and for one to move to this degree, they must participate in the Great rite and ritual flagellation. They can perform the great rite either symbolically or actually, depending on their feelings about the rite. When someone holds this degree, he can create autonomous covens of any parent coven.

Robert Cochrane developed the Cochranian tradition, and this Wiccan practice does not have varying degrees of initiation. It, however, has various stages that depict whether an individual is a novice or not. Some Wiccans also self-initiate themselves if they want to dedicate their lives to practice Wicca.

Handfasting

Wiccans also hold this celebration, which is similar to a Christian wedding. Some Wiccan traditions also allow couples to try staying married for a year and one day. These traditions state that the marriage must begin on Lammas and end a year and day after Lammas. They follow this since this was a traditional time for trial marriages in Ireland. One of the common vows in Wicca is "for as long as love lasts." Wiccans do not use the traditional vow, "till death do us part" when they get married. The first-ever Wiccan wedding was between Frederic Lamind and Gillian, his first wife. Their marriage took place in 1960 when they were a part of the Bricket Wood coven.

Wiccaning

Most Wiccan families perform the Wiccaning ritual, which involves babies, and this is synonymous with Christening. The objective of this rite is to present the baby to the

Goddess and God to ask for their protection. Since Wicca is a tradition that people can freely follow, the child does not necessarily have to follow the same path as his parents.

The Great Rite

The Great rite is often a ritual that symbolizes sexual intercourse or is ritual sexual intercourse. In the former version, the High Priest sends the ritual knife or Athame (which represents men) into a chalice or cup (which represents women). This chalice is filled with red wine and is held by the High Priestess. This rite symbolizes the union of the Lover God and the Maiden Goddess and is also called the fertility rite.

Numerous ritual occasions call for this rite to be performed, especially during Beltane, which occurs around November 1 in the Southern Hemisphere and May 1 in the Northern Hemisphere. This is often performed by the High Priest and Priestess, but others may also be a part of this rite.

Wicca Symbols and Signs

In Wicca, some symbols are used to represent the elements, while others are used to represent an idea. This section covers some of the commonly used symbols.

Air

Air is a classical element; it is the Element of the East, and it is invoked often in Wiccan rituals. According to Wiccan philosophies, the air is connected to the breath of life and the soul. This symbol is often associated with the colors white and yellow. In some traditions and cultures, the air is represented as a triangle, which is a masculine symbol or element. In other Wiccan traditions, the air is represented by a leaf-like image, a feather, or a circle with a point in the center. In other traditions, a triangle is not used to represent air but is used to represent the initiation rank or the association degrees that a practitioner has with the coven. This symbol is also used in alchemy, but the horizontal line extends beyond the triangle's vertices.

If you perform any rituals or cast a spell where you need to call the air element, use the triangle symbol, incense, a fan, or defender. This element is associated with wisdom, power of the mind, and communication. If you must use air, always perform the ritual on a windy day since you can harness the energy in the wind when you cast a spell. You can visualize the currents carrying away any negative energy or thoughts and carrying only positive thoughts and emotions to people who are far away. When you perform a ritual or cast a spell using air, you must embrace the wind. Let the energy fill you and intensify your intentions.

In most traditions using magic, this element is associated with different elemental beings and spirits. Sylphs, or winged creatures, are connected or associated with wind and air. These creatures represent intuition and wisdom. In some beliefs, devas and angels are also associated with air. It is important to note that a deva in new age traditions is not the same as the deva in Hinduism or Buddhism.

Celtic Shield Knot

This symbol is used both for protection and warding. Shield knots have been used in various cultures around the world and have also taken different forms. A shield knot is often represented as a square, and the design ranges from a simple to a complex knot. In the Celtic version of the symbol, a series of knots are used to represent the shield knot. In some cultures, this shield is represented as a square with loops drawn at each of the four corners.

This symbol is commonly used as a tattoo or, in some cases, as a protective talisman. Practitioners in today's Celtic groups invoke it during rituals as a way of keeping negative energy away. In some traditions, elements are represented with the knot; keep in mind that there are only three realms spiritually represented in Celtic tradition – the sea, the earth, and the sky.

While plenty of books have been written about Celtic culture and traditions, you won't find any written records detailing the existence of the Celts in the past.

The Seax Wicca

Raymond Buckland took inspiration from the Saxon religion when he founded the Seax Wicca tradition in 1973. However, you mustn't confuse the two; Seax Wicca is NOT the same as the Saxon tradition. The Seax symbol is used to represent the moon, the sun, and the eight Sabbats and was initially formed as a way of filling Buckland's own religious requirements.

In 1974, Buckland released a book entitled "The Complete Book of Saxon Witchcraft," providing guidance on the tradition. It is interesting to note that, unlike many other Wiccan religions, Seax does not require followers to take an oath of secrecy. Buckland wanted to ensure a more open and democratic experience in an attempt to move away from what he saw as self-gratifying and egotistic traditions. Most covens will elect a high priest or high priestess, and the coven, as a whole, decides when, how, and what to worship. They also allow non-members to come to some rituals, as long as the entire coven is in agreement.

The Sun Wheel

This represents the eight Sabbats that Wiccan traditionalists follow on the Wheel of the Year. The term comes from "solar cross," a calendar used in Europe for the solstices and equinoxes before Christianity was more widely adopted. There are three ways to depict the sun wheel – a circle, a cross with a wheel, and a circle and a dot.

The sun has long been a symbol representing magic and power, and, because of that, the Greeks showed prudence and piety when they honored God. Rather than wine, many Greeks preferred to give an offering of honey to the sun, believing that it was bad for the sun to become intoxicated. Because they believed that the sun was all-powerful, intoxication would lead to the sun's heat and energy destroying all life.

Something similar was used by the Egyptians, differentiating the God of Light from all the other deities by drawing the symbol above him. Invoking the sun during a ritual involved visualizing light to the east. Most of the time, this tradition is celebrated on the Midsummer Solstice and the Return at Yule Festival.

The Triple Moon

Often called the "triple goddess," this symbol is representative of the three moon phases – full moon, waxing, and waning. It has also been said, although this is somewhat questionable, that the symbol represents the three womanhood phases – maiden, mother, and crone.

The triple moon symbol represents the goddess in many traditions, including Wicca. The three crescents represent:

- The first crescent – the waxing moon, associated with new beginnings, new life, rejuvenation.

- The second crescent – the full moon, associated with the highest potency of magic, the recommended time for casting the strongest spells.

- The third crescent – the waning moon, the best time for banishing magic to be performed. This design is commonly seen in pieces of jewelry.

The Triquetra

Much like the triskele, the triquetra is a series of three overlapping arcs in a kind of triangular pattern. It is typically seen in Ireland representing the Holy Trinity, but it's fair to say that it's a much older symbol than many of the Christian traditions. It is thought to date back to around 500 BC, one of the oldest symbols, when it was used as a symbol for the triple goddess. It is known in some traditions as the Rune of Protection and symbolizes Earth, Air, and Water.

Today, thy symbol is popular in jewelry, knotwork, emblems, and so on, where a tri-fold symbol is needed – life, death, and rebirth, love, honor, protect, and so on. Often, a circle is interlaced into the triquetra, indicating the bond that ties the elements.

This symbol is referred to as a Celtic symbol but is also used in various Nordic traditions. Historians have found this symbol on Germanic coins and on runestones in Sweden. There is a strong similarity between this symbol and the valknut design used in the Norse traditions, and the latter represents Odin. This symbol has been found in various Celtic artworks and in the Book of Kells. It often appears in jewelry and metalwork. This symbol never appears by itself, and historians and researchers speculate that this symbol was first created to only use as a filler to fill up a blank space.

This symbol may also appear within a circle and is also represented as a circle that has three overlapping sections. Most Wiccans use this symbol as a power of three. They believe this symbol represents the magical abilities of three witches, and they derived this belief from the Television Series Charmed.

Water

Water is one of the four classical elements, and this is feminine energy. It is connected closely with the goddess. In some Wiccan traditions, especially the British coven, water is used to represent the second degree of initiation. The inverted triangle is used to represent water, and this is a feminine symbol. This symbol is closely associated with the shape of the womb. Some traditions also represent water as horizontal crossbars within a circle or a series of wavy lines.

Since water is connected to the West, it is related to purification and healing. Western traditions use holy water, which is regular water with salt, in any spiritual ritual or path. Salt is another symbol of purification. In most covens, saltwater is always used to protect the circle and the objects or symbols placed on the altar.

Most traditions and cultures use water spirits in their mythology and folklore. In Greek mythology, a water spirit, known as a naiad, presides over a stream or spring. Romans also had a similar entity in their religion. If you want to practice divination, you can use water for scrying at the time of the full moon. Ellen Dugan, the author of elements of witchcraft, suggested that it is best to meditate if you want to communicate with water spirits. It is also best to use waters in various rituals that involve fluid emotions, like love. Some practitioners prefer to cast a spell near a stream or river. You should let the current carry away any negative emotions or thoughts you want to be rid of.

Yin Yang

This symbol represents spirituality and is more influenced by Eastern cultures than contemporary Wicca or Pagan. This symbol does require some mentioning since you can find it across the world, and this is one symbol most people recognize. This symbol represents the polarity of every being in the universe and is often used to represent balance. Black and white are the equal portions of the symbol, and each is surrounded by a circle of the opposing color. This shows there is balance in the various forces in the universe. This symbol represents the balance between dark and light or a link between two opposite forces.

Some cultures place the white portion on top while others place it at the bottom. The symbol finds its origins in Chinese symbols, but it is also used in Buddhism to represent the rebirth cycle. This symbol is also used in Taoism and symbolizes the Tao itself. It is also known as Taiji.

The Yin Yang symbol is traditionally Asian, but many similar images have been found across the globe. Some Roman centurions have also used this symbol. That said, there is no evidence to connect the images from the Roman Empire to those found in the eastern world.

It is best to use this symbol if you want to perform rituals where you must call for harmony or balance. If you want polarity in your life, use this symbol as your guide. You can also use this symbol if you are on a quest for spiritual rebirth. In some traditions, this symbol is described as the valley and a mountain. As the sun climbs over the mountain, the valley is illuminated because of the sunlight. When the sun faces the opposite side, the mountain loses light, and so does the valley. Visualize the shift in sunlight when you use the symbol to cast a spell.

Chapter Three: Types of Magic

White Magic

Most practitioners divide magic into two types – white magic and black magic. The former is also known as the right-hand path, while the latter is known as the left-hand path. The definition of these forms of magic is often debated, but the one commonly accepted is that white magic is associated with healing and positivity, while black magic only represents harm and negativity. Some also believe that white magic is used for a good while black magic is always done to appease the spell caster. Regardless, the actual practice of both forms of magic is dependent on the belief system, individual practitioners, and schools of thought.

Setting up the Altar

Pick the Base

You can position your altar on a flat surface or raised surface. Ensure the altar is wide enough to accommodate your ritual items and your Book of Shadows. You can use a nightstand, coffee table, large storage chest, or a shelf. Some practitioners prefer to use a round altar since it is easy for them to move around the table when they cast their spells. Others prefer rectangular or square altars since it is easy to store the items. It is recommended that you choose an altar made of wood or any other material found in nature.

Identify the Spot

You must always pick the spot where it is generally quiet since you need to concentrate when you cast a spell. Some

Wiccan traditions state that the altar must always be placed facing either the East or North, but the direction depends on the school of thought. Always place the altar in a spot where there is natural light. You can place the altar in a spot you believe is positive or associated with creation.

Arrange the Symbols

When you set up the altar, you must place the necessary symbols around the altar. These symbols help to centralize the energy in the objects. The items you use can represent Mother Goddess or the Horned God. You can also use personal deities of your choice. Some practitioners choose to use different colored candles to represent the elements of deities, while others purchase figures to represent them. Some practitioners, however, pick items that give meaning to their beliefs, and these items are derived from traditions and myths.

Represent the Elements

Most traditions use different symbols to represent the four elements, and these symbols are arranged around the altar. Place the symbols as per their cardinal directions. When you perform white magic, you should use light or white colored items to represent the elements.

Casting Spells

Always Determine Your Intent

Make sure to have a clear goal in mind when you always cast a spell or perform a ritual. Always remember that white magic is positive, and it does not harm anybody. This form of magic encourages happiness, growth, peace, healing, etc. Most people believe that white magic does not give the spell caster power over the other person. When you follow this tenet, you must never cast a love spell where you force someone to fall for you or love you. Instead, use the white magic to attract an unknown person instead of using the spell to force someone to fall in love with you. Some of the spells in the fifth chapter in this book ask you only to visualize the ideal partner for you and then cast the spell.

Select Objects to Enhance Your Spell

You can use different objects to cast your spell. You can use different items that are personal to you or have some meaning. Always draw from your covens or cultural symbols and traditions when you cast a spell. You can also use specific figurines and herbs to strengthen your spell. Do not overcrowd your altar when you perform a spell. When you cast a white magic love spell, you must represent the qualities you look for in a partner around your altar. You can add a dash of spice or pepper to the altar if you want someone who is passionate. Represent intelligence using the statue of an owl. You can also use saffron to represent an individual who is stable or happy.

Cast Your Protective Circle

As mentioned in the first chapter, you must create a protective circle around yourself when you cast a spell. Create this circle around the altar and stand in the center before you cast a spell. You can use a string, stones, salt, twigs, chalk, or other objects to draw the circle. Cast your spell by facing the altar.

Meditate

The objects you put on your altar can be used in meditation, as a way of clearing your mind of negativity. Meditation is the best way to ensure you can focus on your intent when casting spells. Your energy can be channeled using a wand or knife, and your focus should be on a certain object on the altar. Try to relate every object to the spell you are casting and say a prayer, calling on the deities or elements to help you.

Use the Right Words

Spell-casting and rituals require you to use the right words in your incantations. There's no need to use an actual spell every time; just pick the words that match your intent. If you want to use spells, do plenty of research before you start, or approach an experienced practitioner for help. Once you have some experience, you can start writing your own spells, transcribing them into your own Book of Shadows.

Whatever spell you intend to cast, memorize it first. If you have to keep stopping to read the words, it won't work. Also, be careful never to perform a spell or ritual that could result in violence, use any negative phrases, or hateful words.

Red Magic

We've all heard of black magic and white magic, but what about red magic? It does exist and is often referred to as "sex" magic. A late Roman exorcist, Gabriele Amorth, published a book titled "An Exorcist Explains the Demonic," describing red magic as "sorcery that influences sentiment and the sphere of sexuality."

Termed as "hoodoo" in some American and African cultures, red magic actually has a much simpler explanation. It is the most basic magic used in many practicing communities, enlightening practitioners to the fact that all of us have magic within us; our bodies are merely the vessel, the medium with which we communicate with the so-called 'real world.'

The reason red magic became known as sex magic was that, typically, two people would cast the spells. These would have been lovers, or two people married to one another. The spells were usually cast to join their minds, bodies, and spirits by giving their souls to one another. This could only be done through sex, which is how red magic got its reputation as sex magic. However, it should be borne in mind that this is not strictly true as the two people did not have to be lovers; they could be friends or acquaintances of the same or opposite sex. The only requirement was that the two people were connected spiritually.

The 'hoodoo' term was derived from what is considered the most powerful magic on earth, voodoo. This was practiced by Africans who were taken, as slaves, to America, a place that knew little about voodoo, only that it was a type of religion practiced by these people. Red magic was seen as being much the same as voodoo, simply because of the ritual sacrifices and offerings made before a spell was cast.

Right now, there is little information recorded about red magic, but the belief is that it started back in medieval times.

Black Magic

Black magic has always been seen as the evil magic, dark magic used for purely selfish or evil reasons, You can see white and black magic as two sides to a path, with the black magic being on the left, dark and malevolent, while the white magic shines on the right side of the path.

Black magic can be traced thousands of years back, as can white magic. Where we can draw parallels between white magic and shamanism, in that both attempted to become close to spiritual beings, black magic was used to invoke the same spirits but for the selfish benefit of the person performing the ritual. These days, black magic is still associated with that and also with evil, with many people believing it is used only to harm others, to bring about their destruction.

Black magic isn't just about intent, though. It's about the tools you use to perform it. They tend to be hot, pointed, and caustic. Practitioners use personal things from their intended victim, such as blood, or hair, and black magic spells are typically cast at night. Practitioners may also ask an underworld demon to help them.

Voodoo has long been associated with black magic, but much of this comes down to movies and books that aren't factually correct. In fact, voodoo has a history all of its own, traditions that have very little association with modern magic and witchcraft. However, because of their use of magic associated with poison, zombies, and curses, voodooists now have an unenviable association with black magic.

Protection Against Black Magic

If you fear being targeted by black magic, there are several protective objectives you can use. These include certain crystals and spells you can cast against negative energy. We'll look more at these later.

Chapter Four: The Book of Shadows

A book of shadows is the book you write your spells and rituals in. That's the simple explanation, but there is a bit more to it. It's your guidebook, as it were, a book containing the basic practices, philosophy, rituals, and Wiccan ethics, as well as your own personal rituals and spells. In some Wiccan traditions, the Book of Shadows passes from one coven member to another, and the high priest or priestess will handwrite rituals and spells, copying them from the initiating witch. If you are initiated into a coven, you will then copy those spells and rituals, from the high priest or priestess's book into yours. You, and you alone, are responsible for maintaining your Book of Shadows.

But where did the Book of Shadows start? A Wiccan by the name of Gerald Gardener claims he created the first book, around the 1940s to 1950s, using it in the Bricket Wood Coven he created. He claims to have said to the coven that the Book was his own book of spells and rituals that he found had worked and offered to let others cop or change them as they saw fit.

But Gardner didn't work alone, enlisting the help of Doreen Valiente, a high-priestess. Over the years, many attempts have been made to keep this original Book of Shadows a secret, but, over the years, it has been republished several times under different names.

The Rewriting

In 1953, Valiente joined the coven at Bricket Lane, and it didn't take long before she became the high priestess. Gardner had originally claimed that the material in his Book of Shadows had come from ancient sources. Still, it didn't take Valiente long to realize that much of it had come from more recent sources, such as "The Gospel of the Witches," "Key of Solomon," and from famed occultist, Aleister Crowley, among other places. When Valiente talked to Gardner about this, he admitted it and told her to rewrite the book herself if she thought she could do a better job. She took him up on that challenge, removing anything that came from or was related to Crowley, given the negativity surrounding his reputation, and writing it as she thought it should be.

British Traditional Wicca

In some forms of British Traditional Wicca, the book of shadows is used by those practitioners who adhere to the Wiccan Rede. British Traditional Wicca includes the following covens – Gardnerian Wicca, Algard Wicca, and Alexandrian Wicca. Practitioners use the book written by Valiente and Gardner. Gardner wrote his book along with Doreen Valiente, and this book included information from numerous modern sources. This book also included various sections written in different styles and included information about witches who were tortured and killed for performing witchcraft. Gardner claimed these sections were historical, and witches were never allowed to write in their book of shadows only until the late early 1900s when people began to accept the uses of magic. He believed that was the reason why most witches avoided writing in their book. When people accepted the use of the book of shadows, many witches began to write various rituals and spells in their personal books. They, however, jumbled the order of the rituals and steps to prevent any novice from using them. Scholars and researchers, however, doubt the authenticity of this information.

According to research, Gardner told his subsequent followers to copy the book word for word. He also told people that Wiccans descended from Monique Wilson, Eleanor Bone, and Patricia Crowther.

Contemporary Usage

Some traditional practitioners maintained two books of shadow. The first book is used to maintain the core rituals that do not change. The second book is used for rituals used by the coven. An initiate, someone who just joined the coven, was allowed to copy rituals from either book. The second book is maintained only by the coven with rituals and practices that the coven must follow. This book differs from one group to the next, but covens do share some information with each other. Some practitioners also maintain a personal book of shadows in addition to the other books. They use this book for personal use and do not pass it on to anybody else.

Publication

After Gardner passed away, Charles Cardell, his rival, published most of the material he found in the book of shadows written by Gardner. Stewart Farrar and Janet Farrar, who were Alexandrians, decided to publish the Gardnerian book in its true form. They obtained Doreen Valient's permission before they published the book in 1984. This book was titled 'The Witches' Way.'

Non-Traditional Wicca

Eclectic or nontraditional forms of Wicca or other neo-Pagan practices, practitioners use the book of shadows to describe a personal Journal. According to these traditions, the witch describes or journals various rituals, spells, and the results of those rituals and spells. They do not pass this book from teacher to student. Now, the book of shadows is maintained electronically. It is not always a handwritten book. Some witches or practitioners still use the book of shadows to record various spells, but they call it the book of mirrors since it contains their experiences, thoughts, and feelings.

Representation in Popular Culture

Charmed, a television fantasy series, features the book of shadows. According to this television show, this book contains arcane law and various spells. It also has the ability to defend itself from any negative energy or harm. The craft, a 1996 film, was a major influence on the charming television series. In this movie, the book was referred to as a diary maintained by the witch. The witch always wrote down power thoughts in this book.

The sequel of the Blair witch project was titled book of shadows. There was, however, a new mention of this book during the film. Critics believe that the title was used as an attempt to capitalize on the established audience of the charming TV series.

What You Should and Shouldn't Write in Your Book

As a Wiccan, you will have many different supplies, but the most important is your Book of Shadows. No coven member will have the exact same spells, rituals, or other information in their book because it is an intensely personal item. And that is also why your Book of Shadows should be kept hidden from all other eyes but your own.

What all this means is that you can pretty much write what you want in your Book, but I will give you some ideas on what should and shouldn't be in there. Trust me when I say that, later down the line, you will find your Book fulfilling if you put the right things in it and leave the wrong things out.

What Should Be in There

Your Name

This goes without saying, really; as the book is yours, make sure you own it with your name.

Your Wiccan Tradition

You should include your beliefs, the path you follow, and what sort of Wiccan you are.

The Wiccan Rede

This binds all Wiccan traditions together. Most religions are full of commandments and laws, but Wiccans bow to just two – the Threefold law, which says that whatever you do in life comes back to you three times over and the Wiccan Rede, which says, "An it harm none, do as ye will."

Your Personal Deities

The deities you choose are personal, particularly when you practice alone, and you must choose the ones that you have a connection with, that you truly believe in. Write the name of the deity in your Book, the name of their pantheon, what meaning they have for you, and any other information.

Your Rituals and Spells

These are all the rituals you like to do, those that you have created by yourself, and the ones that you want to try in the future. Do the same for the spells – all the ones you tried and loved, those you created and those you want to try. When you write each one, include as much information as you can, such as the recipes so you can have everything ready when you next perform it.

The Sabbats and Rituals

Write each Sabbat down and write what the seasons mean for you. List the rituals you like to do during the Sabbats you listed and state how your altar is decorated for each particular Sabbat.

Specific Correspondence Charts

This includes your crystal chart, herbal correspondence

chart, and your candle color chart. Your Book of Shadows is much like a reference book and, having all the important stuff written in one place means you don't need to keep piles of books that will end up being thrown away at some point.

Your Thoughts, Your Reflections, and Your Experiences

You should also consider your Book of Shadows as a kind of diary or a journal, and you should write down everything relevant along your spiritual journey. When you look back over it, you can see your mindset at any given time, your realizations, and so on, Don't be shy about what you write; it is for your eyes only.

Your other Wiccan supplies, such as altar patens, smudge bowls, candles, etc., can be replaced, but your Book of Shadows cannot. You have no chance of rewriting it all as it was, and you can't relive the experiences you had in the past.

What Shouldn't Be in Your Book

While there are things that definitely should be in your Book of Shadows, by the same token, there are things that should not. The idea of your Book is to record your journey, both spiritual and magickal. It is a Book you can look back on in years to come, and you don't want to read anything negative, or you don't want your daughters to read anything negative when you pass it onto them.

What you shouldn't include in your book are:

Things That Are Not Connected With Magick or Wicca

This is your personal account of your own spiritual Wiccan journey, not your household chores list, grocery list, or a place to sort out your household bills. It is for you to write you rituals, spells, thoughts, dreams, etc., that are all related to Wicca.

Hate-Filled Thoughts

Lots of people are tempted to write things down in the heat of the moment, bad thoughts they may have about a partner or someone else. Yes, this is a great way to let off some steam, but keep those thoughts out of your Book of Shadows. You can always start a separate journal for that sort of thing if it makes you feel better. You will only regret it later down the line when you look through your Book and find it filled with hatred and negative thoughts. At the end of the day, negativity can fade out of your life; writing it in your Book of Shadows only keeps it alive forever.

Hexes and Curses

Wicca is white, not black magick; it's about purity and shining lights. Wicca is a peaceful religion, based on a lover of nature and very grounded. It isn't about black curses and hexes, and it isn't about abandoning the Divine. Don't forget the threefold law and the Wiccan Rede; if you start dabbling in curses, you won't be on the right side of the Divine.

Entries From Someone Else

What that means, of course, is that you shouldn't allow anyone else to write their entries in your Book of Shadows. Keep your own Book, and keep it just for you. Don't even let anyone else read it, let alone write in it. If a friend has thoughts of their own that they want to write down, tell them to get a Book of their own, and don't give in to pressure.

As you can see, there is much you can write in your book and little that you shouldn't. Stick to these guidelines and your Book of Shadows will be perfect for you. You will be able to go back through it in the years to come, see how far you progressed, how much you achieved along the way. And when you pass it on to your daughter or your granddaughter, you are passing on a Book you are proud of.

Chapter Five: Love and Relationship Spells

I am not too sure what you may have in your kitchen cupboard at the moment, so this chapter has some simple love spells you can use. You will definitely have the ingredients needed to cast these spells.

Red Candle Spell

To perform this spell, you need the following:

- Red yarn or ribbon

- Two Red taper candles

- Candle dressing

- Sharp knife or carving tool

Follow the steps given below to cast this spell:

- The first step is to dress the candles. Write or carve your name and your partner's name on separate candles. You can also carve a desired outcome or petition to perform this spell. Cleanse the candles and then dress them however you want to purify them. Now, set your intention for the spell on the candles

- The next step is to bind the candles, and you can do this using the ribbon or yarn. You can tie seven knots, but always choose a number you resonate with. Set the intention while you tie the knots. It can be as simple as, "With this knot, I bind us together in love."

- The last step is to light the candles, and, as you are now bound together, you must bring your intention into the spell. Let the candles burn until they go out naturally, or the candle melts fully. You can dress the altar or plate with candles with different love items, such as sugar, honey, rose petals, etc. You can also use tarot cards when these candles burn.

Ribbon Spell

To cast this spell, you need the following:

- Red or pink ribbon

- Pepper and saltshakers, or any other objects that make a pair, such as your favorite shoes, a set of bookends, etc.

Follow the steps given below to cast this spell:

- Wait for the New Moon to conduct this spell.

- Pick the objects. It is important to note that one of the objects represents you, while the other represents your partner.

- Now, take the ribbon and bind the two together and leave some space between the two.

- Untie the ribbon every morning, and move the objects closer to each other and retie the knot.

- Do this until the objects touch each other.

- Now, leave the shoes tied together for a few more days or until you meet your new love.

Rose Spell

To cast this spell, you will need the following:

- A source of moving water, preferably a river, ocean or stream, but if you do not live close to any water body, use the washbasin or bathtub

- Rose Petals

To cast this spell, follow the steps given below:

- The first thing you must do is to visualize the person whom you desire to be your lover or partner.

- Now, collect the petals of a rose and throw them to the water while you chant the following: "As this rose flows out to waters so that true love will find me."

- Repeat this process twice and make sure to visualize your dream lover.

- Always throw the petals so that the water brings them back to you to ensure the Universe knows you need love to come to you.

Fairy Love Spell

When you want to draw new love, you should start planting red primroses in your garden. So, go to the local nursery and buy a few red primroses. Pot them and place them either near your front or backdoor. Every night touch the pot with both hands and gaze at the plants. Focus all your energy on the flowers and say the following:

"Flower of love, realm of the fey,

Bring me a lover before it is May."

Repeat the spell every Friday until you find your true love. When this happens, thank the flower and place a shiny dime in the pot. Then snip one blossom from the pot and slip that into a muslin bag. Leave the bag near your clothes and pin it close to your heart when you get dressed for work or go out. When you do this, observe the feelings associated with love and feel them deeply. Visualize the love you want to attract. When you tend to the flowers regularly and devote yourself to keeping the plant alive, you will soon find your true love. When your spell succeeds, share a drink with your partner and offer the first glass to the flower.

Love Poppet

A love or spell poppet uses the principles of sympathetic magic. Sympathetic magic is a form of magic based on the idea that when you perform an action on any object, that action affects everything that the object represents. These poppets are often referred to as Voodoo dolls, but they are not bad objects to use. The term is a misnomer since Voodoo represents a set of religious traditions followed in West Africa, and this culture is prevalent in Caribbean and Louisiana populations. Voodoo dolls do not have too much prominence in either of these traditions, but they appear in numbers of magical traditions across the globe.

The Western culture, unfortunately, demonizes voodoo dolls and taints the beautiful, complex, and rich traditions of voodoo itself. It is for these reasons we use the term poppet to represent this doll. This doll is not used to torture the target, and you do not have to poke it with needles. It is used to draw money, power, luck, and love. For this spell, you must create a poppet that represents the person you love.

Tips for This Spell Poppet Tutorial

It is easy to make your poppet, and if you know how to thread the needle and use scissors, you are sorted. There are some issues you must note when it comes to stitching.

Do not fear, because this section will help you prevent any mistakes that people often make.

1. Do not try to keep the stitches inside the poppet, since that will not work. If you want to stitch inside the poppet, you need a very large poppet.

2. Use the whip stitch

Do not panic if you do not know these stitches. They are extremely easy to learn.

Choosing a Fabric

It is best to work with cotton quilting fabric since it is easy to stitch them. You can customize the spell any way you need, depending on what you want from life. For this spell, let us choose a rose print since roses represent romance, love, and attraction. The mileage you choose may vary, but it would be best to choose a cool blue fabric if you want a healing poppet and a green one to attract wealth or money. You can do as you please.

To do this, you need the following:

- Love herbs like lavender, rosemary and dried roses

- Sturdy scrap paper or cardstock. You can also use cardboard or cereal boxes

- 1/8 yard quilting fabric, preferably cotton

- Matching thread

- Scissors

Follow the steps given below to make your poppet:

Step 1

Fold the cardstock and draw the outline of the shape of the goddess. You can use any shape you like to depict the goddess.

Step 2

Cut the shape of your choice and open it. Place it directly on the fabric you want to use and cut two pieces of fabric using that shape.

Step 3

Now, place the incorrect sides of the poppet together, but do not sew it yet. Turn the sides out unless you want to make a large poppet. You can use a basic whipstitch around the edges, but leave an opening at the bottom of the poppet.

Step 4

Now, add a little fiber or cotton to the poppet to fill it. Do this only if you want it to be plush. Do not add stones or cotton since that will not help you during the spell. You can use a combination of the following herbs:

- Lavender

- Rosemary

- Orange peel

- Dried apple peel

- Dried roses

Now, sew the opening of the poppet.

Step 5

You are finally ready to charge the poppet. Let us first do some quick clearing of energy from the poppet. You can do any of the steps mentioned below to charge the poppet with energy:

- Leave the poppet near your window and let it bask in the moonlight

- Sleep with the poppet close to your pillow for at least seven nights

- Make a circle with candles and place the poppet in between the candles for a few hours You can also use any other method you like to charge the poppet

Kiss the Moonlight - A Strong Love Charm

The moon is incredibly powerful, as it the light that shines from it, especially when you want to perform magic. That power works well for any love spells, including this one.

You will need

- Red or pink rose petals

- Piece of rose quartz

- A small bowl of silver

You must perform this ritual at night, preferably on the day of the new moon. This means you cannot view the moon at night. Kiss the crystal and put it into the bowl. Now sprinkle the rose petals over the stone and place the bowl close to the window. Leave the bowl near the window for seven days. Once seven days have passed, pick up the crystal and use it, drawing romance and love to you. The bowl can now be placed near to the window, with the petals in it, until another full moon arrives.

Love Star

The Love Star spell must be cast on a clear night when all the stars are out. Gather the ingredients listed below and position yourself close to a wide-open window so that you can see the stars:

You will need:

- A red candle
- Jasmine incense stick
- Pink or red crystals, like Carnelian, Garnet, or a Rose Quartz

Place the candle and the incense stick on your altar and light both of them. Focus on the brightest star you can see in the sky and gather the crystals into your hands. Close your eyes, visualize the light from that bright star filling the crystals and say the following words, three times:

Star of love, burn so bright Aid me in my spell tonight
Unite my true love to me As I will it, so mote it be.

After the third incantation, put the crystals onto your altar, close to your candle, and leave the candle and incense to burn out by themselves.

As Friday's ruler is the goddess of love, Venus, these spells should be cast on that day. You can be particular about your timing if you want to be, and wait for the crescent or new moon to cast the spells. During those moons, the energy is positive, creative, and it helps in attracting newness to you.

A Love Pouch With a Magnetic Lodestone

This is the absolute best stone for this purpose as magnetic lodestones are known for symbolizing attraction. Use natural lodestones where you can, but if you cannot find them, you can use small magnets to cast this spell. You also need:

- Love drawing oil

- 1 small red bag

You can either use a purchased blend of oils designed for love spells or make your own oil. Use a mixture of ylang-ylang, rose, cardamom, ginger, and vanilla oils to create a potent love blend. Add a few drops to your palm and rub them. Now, rub the lodestones to anoint them with the loving blend. Continue to rub the stones until your palms are warm. Now, concentrate on the stones and draw romance and love into your life. Drop the stones into the bag and continue to rub the bag in your hands. Let some of the oil stick to the bag as well. Now, place this bag near your bedside table or in your bag to attract your true love.

Chapter Six: Money and Wealth Rituals

Now that we have looked at the various spells and rituals to bring love into your life, let us look at some rituals to help you bring in more wealth and money.

Rice Ritual

You should only perform this ritual when you know nobody is going to visit your home. If you want, you can ask for the Archangel Uriel to help you when you perform this spell, so nobody interrupts your ritual. When you perform this ritual with a strong belief and intent, you will see the results sooner than expected.

To perform this ritual, you need the following ingredients:

- Rice

- Two glass jars with lids

- Six grains of black pepper

- Two green candles

To perform the ritual, follow the steps given below:

- Place the jars and lids in boiling water to sterilize them, and then dry them properly.

- Place a handful of rice in both jars and add three gains of pepper above the rice. Now, seal the jars.

- Place one jar in the dining room and the other in the

kitchen. If you do not have a separate dining room, you can place both on opposite sides of the kitchen. Make sure you place the jars in an area that is easily visible to you.

• Place one candle in front of each jar and light it. Let the candle burn for two hours before you wave them out.

• Discard the candles and leave the jars in the same area for the next time you perform this ritual.

An Abundance of Money Ritual

Using nothing more than sugar and gold coins, you can attract money to you easily. The combination of sugar and coins creates the energy required to attract money. Choose a Thursday night or the crescent moon for this ritual.

You will need:

- Three gold coins
- Some white sugar
- A wide-mouthed clear glass jar
- A smaller glass to go inside the big one
- Red ribbon

Here's how to do this ritual:

- Pour sugar into the large jar, filling it up
- Put the small glass inside the large glass and twist it to set it firmly into the sugar
- The coins go into the small jar and then the red ribbon is tied around the large jar
- As you are doing all this, say these words, over and again – "Abundance of money."
- When you have completed this, stand facing the main door to the house
- Place your glass jars just inside the door on the left-hand side. Make sure it is not where it can be kicked or knocked over when people come through the door.

Water Ritual

This ritual is designed to attract enough money to you to last the whole month and requires just two simple ingredients – a glass of water and two heaped tablespoons of table salt or sea salt.

- On the first Sunday in the month, fill up a glass with water – tap or bottled water, either will do. Add one tablespoon of salt and leave it for one hour
- Pour the salt water over your hands, washing them thoroughly. Say the words, "Salt is my protector; it will make money multiply, so my home lacks for nothing."
- Leave your hands to dry naturally, not with a towel or anything else
- Add the rest of the salt to another glass of water
- Place it in one corner of a room in your house and leave it for 24 hours – it will absorb the negative energy swirling around
- Pour the contents of the glass away after 24 hours and sit back and watch the money come to you throughout the month.

Green Candle Money Ritual

You need to perform this ritual five days before the day you are to receive the money since it takes five days to complete it. This is a great ritual that helps you manifest some money. Before you perform the ritual, you must think about the money you need and visualize that it is already in your account.

To perform this ritual, you need the following:

- Peppermint oil

- One green pillar candle

- One white sheet of paper

- One silver coin

To perform this ritual, follow the steps given below:

- Write the amount of money you need on the piece of paper.

- Smear or rub the candle with the oil using your hands

- Place the coin on one side of the candle and draw a dollar sign using the edge of the coin.

- Now, light the candle and think about the money you need, and visualize it coming into your home for at least ten minutes.

- Fold the paper with the amount you need to be written on it. Fold it thrice lengthwise and three more times to form a square. You should have an envelope in your hand.

- Place the coin inside the envelope and seal it using the wax from the candle.

- Now hold the envelope close to your chest and say the following, "Money I need come to me." Chant this spell however many times you would like to, but say it as you mean it

- Now, place the envelope under the candle holder and let the candle burn for another twenty minutes. Wave the candle out with your hand and do not blow it out

- Continue the ritual for the next five days by lighting it every morning and focusing on your intent.

Pumpkin Spice For More Cash

This ritual is one of the best ways to expand your income. You can use this if your income often depends on a bonus program or commission. The only ingredient you need to perform this ritual is one large can of pumpkin spice. Follow the steps given below to perform this ritual:

- Put some money aside five days before you are due to get paid and sprinkle it with pumpkin spice. Now, wave the wad of cash in front of the main door to your house.

- Five days or more before you are due to get paid, sprinkle your shoes with more pumpkin spice.

That is all you need to do. Now, look for any opportunities where you can get a bigger paycheck. The ingredients used to make pumpkin spice are a mix of those that attract money. If you want to make your own mix, use the spices and herbs listed below:

- Cloves

- Thyme

- Nutmeg

- Ginger

- Allspice

- Basil

- Cinnamon

Pay a Bill

Cast this spell if there is a specific debt or bill you must pay, and you are not looking only for general prosperity. To perform this spell, you need the following:

- Cinnamon oil or patchouli
- Incense
- A piece of paper
- Green candle

To cast this spell, follow the steps given below:

- Use the pen to draw some symbols to represent the bill on the paper. You can use logos, words, dollar figures, or any other symbols that represent the bill. Since you will burn this paper, do not use a real bill. You can use a photocopy of a dollar bill to cast this spell. That said, it is best to use your own drawing as it has a kind of energy associated with it.

- Smear or rub the candle with the oil and place the paper under the holder. Now, light the incense and candle and repeat the following while you watch the flames:

"The candle burns

And lights the way

For money coming

This bill will pay"

- Focus on the bill and why you must pay it off. Let the candle burn for 10 minutes while you visualize yourself paying off the bill. Burn this candle every day for seven days, so make sure the candle is large enough. Remove the candle on the seventh day and burn the paper completely. Let the candle continue to burn until it goes out.

- If you want to honor the spell, put any unexpected earnings towards this bill. Otherwise, you may end up losing the money.

Wealth Attraction Bath

You can use this bath mixture at any time during the day, but it is best to use it before you attend an event where you can earn money. So, use this mixture before a bank visit, a job interview, or a business meeting. All you need to do this are:

- 3 drops pine oil

- 3 drops cinnamon oil

- 3 drops basil oil

- A handful of sea salt

- Small bottle or vial with a tight lid

- A pinch of patchouli herb

Follow the steps given below to use this mixture:

- Run a bath, and when the water is warm, add the herb, salt, and oils to the water.

- Soak in the mixture for at least 15 minutes. While you are in the tub, think about the event and visualize how it may bring money into your life.

- Visualize the outcome you want

- Fill the bottle or vial with the bathwater and place the lid. Now, drain the bath.

- Carry the vial or bottle with you to the meeting.

Welcome Wealth Spell

If you want to welcome wealth and prosperity into your home, you can cast a welcoming spell on the main entrance to your house.

You will need

- A doormat
- Some sandalwood chips
- A small handful of dried patchouli
- A small handful of dried basil
- One Silver Coin

To cast your spell

- Position your doormat outside the main entrance to the house
- When you are happy with the position, lift it and spread the basil, patchouli, and sandalwood beneath it
- Bury the coin within the herbal mixture and place the mat back over the top
- Stand upon your mat and face to the north. Say the following words:

"I welcome wealth to my home.

Please stop here, do not roam.

My welcome mat is here you see

Bring in new prosperity."

Move off the mat. Now welcome wealth opportunities to start flowing in

Chapter Seven: Health and Wellbeing Spells

Energy Spells

When you are feeling low, your morale is all but gone, and you need your spirits to lift you out of the doldrums, try an energy spell. These spells let you tap into the Earth's energy and use it to boost your own. You may not be filled with boundless energy, but you will get enough of a boost so that you can get through the day on a happier note. Here are some of the more popular energy spells.

Relight the Spark

The name says it all here; you want your spirit relit and replenished, and this is the spell to do it. It is one of the simpler spells and provides just enough power to put you back in control.

You will need an orange candle, some orange yarn, a stick of cinnamon, and a heatproof pan or dish. You must have enough yarn to wrap around the candle a few times.

Hold the candle and begin wrapping the yarn around it, making equally spaced knots in it as you go – the knots must all be touching the surface of the candle.

Next, put the candle into a candle holder and prepare your mind, so you are fully focused on the spell. Block out all external distractions, go into your mind, and try to feel the energy that comes from within the earth. You should feel an energy surge, starting from your feet and traveling up your body to your head.

Once your mind and body are filled with this energy, hold it there, and light your cinnamon stick. Repeat the following, out loud, a minimum of four times – "Energy, power, rise up the tower."

Now hold the cinnamon stick to the candle and, when the candle is alight, leave it to burn for a few moments. When the flame is steady, place the candle into the heatproof pan or dish. Focus only on the energy from the fire as it begins to eat away at the wax. Do not allow your focus to become disturbed, and do not break your focus until the candle has burned down entirely.

Crystal Booster Bag

Every day is different, and you can't possibly know what each one will bring. Sometimes you will sail through a day with no trouble while, on others, you might suddenly find yourself in a panic, weighed down with a ton of work or chores that just have to be done right now. With the crystal booster, you can create a spell that you can use at the drop of a hat, a spell to help you when what was a standard steady day, suddenly turns into a hectic mess. This spell will provide you with a boost of strength, the drive you need to power through to the end of the day.

You will need a small blue or white bag made from cloth, some cedarwood chips (or you can just add a few drops of cedarwood oil to standard wood chips), and one each of the following crystals – pyrite, citrine, red jasper, and bloodstone.

There is nothing complicated about this spell; just place all of your ingredients into the cloth bag, and tie it with a tight knot. Place it in your handbag or a bag that you take to work with you every day, and it will help you face the day ahead and cope with any tough parts of the day.

Happiness Spells

You might have heard, somewhere along the way, that you can pull happiness out of nowhere with just a simple happiness spell. Sorry, but it doesn't work that way, and neither can you induce a happy state of mind. What happiness spells do is help you shed off stress, and that should make you happier.

What you must keep in mind that magic isn't a cure and, if your heart isn't in it or your mind isn't in the right place, these spells may not work or may not provide you with the result you want. Happiness spells can give you a bit of a boost if you are feeling a little low, but don't expect them to remove depression or serious, deep-hearted sorrow by themselves. Part of making any spell work, especially happiness spells, is to put the effort in to improve your mood by yourself; if you don't, these spells are unlikely to work.

The primary ingredient for any happiness spell is to ensure your mind is clear and in the right mental place.

Three Candle Joy Spell

This spell is designed to give you a burst of positivity when you are at your lowest ebb. You will need three candles – orange, yellow, or a combination of both – a couple of pinches of dried rosemary or marjoram, and cedar oil.

Apply the cedar oil to the candles and then position them on your altar, Light them in turn and sprinkle your dried herbs around them on the altar. Calm your mind, focus your attention on the heat coming from the candle flames. Stretch your hands over the heat and, when you begin to feel the fire's energy radiating towards you, channel that power, saying the following words aloud -

"Happiness and joy come into my life.

Away with anger, stress, and strife

I am happy; I am free

No more negativity."

Do make sure that you don't get your hands too close to the flame – the last thing you want is to burn them!

Blooming Happiness

A blooming spell takes energy from positive energy vibes given off by flowers. You will some lilac or jasmine oil, any fresh flower, a heatproof dish, a yellow candle, a pencil, and some paper.

Focus your mind on three things that are negatively affecting your happiness. Light your candle and write all these on the paper. Now hold the paper to the candle flame and let it burn to nothing, dropping it in your heatproof container until it burns out. Put a few drops of the oil on the flower, close your eyes, and inhale the scent. As you do, you can see whatever is making you unhappy disappearing, just as the paper turns to ash in the flames. Once you can see that in your mind, drop the flower into the dish, on top of the ash. Leave the dish on your altar as a reminder to yourself to be happy.

Winds of Change

This spell is aimed at attacking whatever causes your unhappiness. It will help to dispel any anxiety and doubts that are stopping you from being happy. For this to work, you need dried basil and dried patchouli, but you also need favorable weather. This is best done on a windy day at the top of a hill. If you don't have hills near you, find a wide-open space where it is windy. Stand in your space and turn your back to the wind. Close your eyes, focus on what is causing you unhappiness and throw the herbs up into the air. As you do, imagine your problems flying away, like the wind carrying the herbs away. Stand still, allow the wind to flow around you, and feel each problem floating away. Say the following words:

"May the winds take my pain.

Make me happy once again.

Then turn around and face the wind. Say:

May the winds bring joy to me.

So that happy I will be'"

Weight Loss

Most of us have, at one time or another, wished we could wave a magic wand, chant a spell, and instantly melt away the excess pounds. Sadly, it just won't happen, and magic doesn't work quite that directly, especially spells for losing weight. The weight loss enchantment is powerful, but it can't work alone. The spell is merely the catalyst that lights the touch paper of your willpower and dedication. To work, you have to focus every ounce of your effort on your weight loss goals.

You must also have the willpower to draw up and stick to a diet plan, to do your daily exercises, because weight loss really isn't magic. It still requires you to burn more calories than you consume; the weight loss spells, provided you follow them carefully, will give you the push you need to be successful, to burn off that fat by sticking to your plan.

The best results come when you use your diet and your exercise regime in conjunction with at least two weight loss spells.

Melt The Pounds Away

This is a simple weight loss spell that should encourage you to stay on the course you have set for yourself. You require nothing more than a brown candle but, because this must be burning for a few nights, try to find the biggest pillar candle you can.

Take a sharp knife and inscribe your current weight onto the candle, near to the top. At the base of the candle, inscribe the weight you want to be. Do make sure you have picked a reasonable amount of weight to lose. Don't, for example, say that you want to lose 50 lbs. where it is only reasonable to expect a loss of 10 lbs. If you are reasonable in your expectations, the results are more likely to be what you want them to be.

Every night, before you go to bed, stand before your altar, and light your candle. Leave it to burn for 15 minutes and focus on your goals. As each day passes, the candle burns down, and, as it does, your own weight will begin to reduce, melting away like the candle wax.

Craving Crystal Spell

This spell can help you to beat those hunger pangs and the cravings that strike when you least expect them. It will help you to turn away from temptations that threaten to derail your good work by breaking your diet. It will keep you tied to your goals. For this spell to work, you need a green candle, some clear quartz, and, if you can get one, a green pouch or cloth bag.

The most important thing about this spell is timing. Choose a waning moon, which occurs around 14 days after the full moon. You should, if you can, cast this spell outside in the moonlight but, if not, choose a large window where you can see the moon. Light your candle, turn your face to the moon, hold the crystal, and say the following words:

"Goddess within

Goddess without

Guide me to my goal

Easy my hunger

Soothe my spirit

Strengthen my resolve

As I wish it, so mote it be."

As you say these words, close your eyes, open your mind, and focus on your goals. Focus on losing those stubborn pounds, convince yourself that you must eat a healthier diet. Think about the foods the tempt you, the unhealthy food choices you crave, and harden yourself against them. Channel the energy you create by doing this to the crystal and continue until you are set in your mind that you will not fall prey to temptation from this moment on.

When you have finished, extinguish the candle. Place the crystal in the small pouch or bag or, if you don't have one, in a pocket or bag that you carry with you all the time. Do not leave the crystal behind; where you go, the crystal goes. When you feel like temptation is in your way, grab the crystal and hold it tight. Draw on the energy it provides to put up a barrier between you and those cravings. Over time, the crystal will help you to develop the will to turn away from temptation and fight off the cravings that you might otherwise fall prey to. As time passes, the crystal will lose its energy, depending on how often you need to use it, so recharge it every month on the waning moon.

Chapter Eight: Magic and the Law of Attraction

Most people have heard of the law of attraction, but many dismiss it as utter rubbish. But it isn't rubbish; it plays a huge part in all our lives and is especially prominent in magic. When you cast a spell, you may not realize that success is largely reliant on that law of attraction, and you will see evidence of that in the results of your spell. Very often, it is the law of attraction that divides two spell casters and their successes.

When you begin to look into the law of attraction, we can see some pretty simple explanations, like your thoughts are all-powerful, and that like will attract like. What it basically means is that if you think about something long enough and often enough, it will eventually become a reality.

This works two ways – you can attract things you want, and you can attract things you don't want. It is habitual thought that attracts things to you and, if you continue to think negative thoughts all the time, all you will succeed in doing is attracting the negativity to you, all those problems and anxieties. By the same token, think positive thoughts all the time, and you will attract positivity to your life.

The law of attraction is backed up by some pretty simple, not to mention natural magic.

- What you think about the most will dictate what your reality is
- What you feel the most will dictate what your reality is
- The law of attraction is very much like the power of gravity, attracting things to you like a strong magnet
- The things you think about are the things you get

- The combination of feelings and thoughts are powerful enough to bring about change in your life
- The law of attraction is how you bring about the reality you want for the future

Thinking on that last point, you might push it aside, saying it isn't true, but it is. You already know, from your magic spells, that the universe is just one big ball of pulsating energy, all at different frequencies, and that energy also exists within you, within all of us. By using the law of attraction, you can make strong connections to the frequencies of the energy attached to what you desire, what you want.

Your thoughts are what fuels the law of attraction. When people say to you, always be careful what you think of, you should listen and avoid thinking of what you don't want. The biggest problem is that our environment and experiences affect what we think. If we are surrounded by negativity or all our experiences are tainted by negativity, then our thoughts follow suit. We tend to focus our thoughts on problems and on all the good stuff that seems to be passing us by; all that does is attract even more negativity.

We must always be aware of our thoughts; we must work at rejecting negativity by thinking only good things. This won't be easy to start with, but if we keep on doing it, we can bring about the right changes.

How to Practice The Law of Attraction

The law of attraction takes some time to understand, but you can start practicing right away; you just have to train your mind in the right way. There are some exercises you can follow to begin attracting things that we want, outcomes we believe we should have. We can break these thought processes into three separate sections – appreciation, affirmation, and then visualization. One of these alone is pretty useless; combine all three, and your results should be spectacular.

By appreciation, we are essentially referring to the feeling of gratitude. It is crucial to acknowledge the facts when things are going rather well for you in the present. By doing this, we make ourselves more aware of all the good things that happen in our lives. When we accept and acknowledge those things, we become more receptive and aware of the positivity around us. Of course, that means we focus lesser on the negativity, and that puts us in a place that allows us to see the bigger picture better.

Affirmation is basically the validation of everything we have appreciated. When we repeat the positive outcomes of the day, it makes us more aware of all the good we have done thus far. That being said, you must also be ready to reaffirm yourself when things do not go according to plan. By doing that, you are giving yourself some much-needed motivation to pick yourself back up and continue on that path against all the odds. While it may seem like a 'fake it till you make it' scenario, many have agreed that this kind of positive outlook and self-motivation have enabled them to reach heights they never thought possible.

Visualization is the easiest one because, at some point in our lives, we have all visualized something. We may have dreamed about the ideal life, the perfect house, the best situations, and so on, but all of them were just parts of the imagination running wild without any purpose other than passing the time. When channeled in tandem with appreciation and affirmation, visualization can also be a powerful tool. In addition to visualizing your dreams in vivid detail, we must also train ourselves to experience the feelings associated with achieving that dream. Once we can visualize those feelings of victor and triumph, it begins fueling the law of attraction and consequently makes our dreams come true. The law of attraction works in its primary form when one has mastered the art of using these three skills together. Such co-ordination will enable them to strengthen their magic beyond their wildest dreams.

Most spell work is built using a combination of appreciation, affirmation, and visualization. Their combined might is manifested as the energy that we witness on the physical plane. While visualization enables you to grasp a fair idea of what is expected, appreciation brings you closer to reality and affirmation rounds off the deal by having you say the spoken word that seals the deal for the enchantment. This is evident from simple spells like lighting a candle all the way up to more complex procedures.

If magic is the art of using energy to bring about the desired effect, then these three things are the tools required to channel that energy effectively. The law of attraction is the simplest way of trying to wrap our heads around the mechanics of magic.

Chapter Nine: Protection Spell

We're going to look at a couple of protection spells that can help you to protect you, and your home.

Protect Yourself

The first protection spell we're going to look at will help you to protect yourself from mental or physical harm dealt by another person. This is one of the most powerful spells you may ever perform, and it can help you throw up a shield between you and a person who won't let go of you, insisting on causing you mental anguish, and between you and other toxic people. This spell can be used to protect you from anything that could be unpleasant but, to ensure the spell remains powerful, you must repeat it several times.

One good thing is that you are not harming anyone when you cast this spell, and you are not manipulating any other person either. When you cast it, remember that you must bring as much energy out of yourself as you can, and draw as much from the earth and the sky as you can. The more energy you can draw on, the more power the spell has, and the longer it will last.

Close your eyes and visualize the person doing you harm is wrapped in a layer of shining energy, a bubble that sounds them and retains their negativity, stopping it from spreading further. That person won't even be able to expel any positive energy; if they think positive thoughts about another person, they will benefit from them and, likewise, if they think negatively about someone, wish them harm, they will be ones to reap that negativity, no-one else.

Light a candle, any color, and visualize that person standing in front of you. If you cannot do that, have a picture of them in front of you instead. Put the picture in front of your candle on the altar and then visualize the bubble around them, repeating the following multiple times:

"All negativity shall now return to you.

All negative you attempt to send me upon you will behold.

All acts, minds, and speech of hate

become your own determined fate. By all

up highest, the earth and wise

By seas wide and lush blue horizons

By night and day, and powers 3

This is mine will and yes it will be.

Harm to non, nor back to me."

Protect Your Home

This next spell involves using positive energy to protect your home and, when the spell is cast, you can bring about a protective shield that surrounds your home. The spell will also help you to fix any imbalances in the energy that surrounds your home, creating a happy and harmonious place for all the people in your house.

A potent spell, its power depends on how well you focus your attention on your intent when casting it. If you are full of anger, anxiety, or feeling tired, wait; do not cast a spell at this time. Wait until your mind is calmer and not full of anxious thought jostling for space. That is the only time you should cast any spell, especially one as powerful as this.

Casting a spell is not easy at the best of times. There are guidelines and rules in place, and we mentioned them right at the start of the book. Follow them for your own safety and peace of mind. Candle spells can also be used to protect your home, and they work similarly to the spell we're going to look at in a minute. Candle spells surround your home in a warm glow, and push energy into the forces protecting your home, keeping negativity and malicious energies away.

You will need:

- A bowl, preferably one that you keep purely for spells

- A teaspoon of garlic powder or minced fresh garlic
- Coarse sea salt or coarse rock salt

Here's how you cast the protective spell:

1. Position the bowl on your altar, at the center
2. Pour the garlic and the salt into it.
3. Mix them together slowly, visualizing your house as a safe place for you and all who live there. Try to visualize the house being cloaked in a protective layer, telling yourself that negative energy cannot get through the layer.
4. When you can see your house in this way, protected from negativity, you should feel the energy leaving your body and flowing into the mix inside of the bowl
5. When you feel that energy, say the following words:

"With this salt, I cleanse this place

Let no one with ill intentions enter this space

Protect this space from all negative energies and entities

So, mote it be."

5. Now carry the mixture with you and place it on every door opening and window in your house. When you travel through your house to seal the negativity from the openings, visualize that the safe energy from the mixture is creating a shield around your house.

6. When you finish sealing the house, that is all the windows and doorways, thank the Universe for protecting you and also your home since you can live there. Let gratitude fill your body and wash away any negativity. Let the feeling of safety and warmth fill you.

Chapter Ten: Other Spells

Healing Spells

Most witches use healing spells, and these are the most commonly used after money and love spells. Most spells for health are tricky since they involve subtle influences when compared to spells used to improve one's financial situation or to find a partner. Doing magic to health, the body will not always be successful since you try to influence some physical conditions in your body. I am talking about physical healing when I say this. Healing spells are different for physical and emotional wounds. For now, let us look at some healing spells you can use for physical healing.

Power of Three

This healing spell uses the number three and the energy and strength associated with that number to heal a physical or emotional wound. This spell is best used when someone is physically ill and not when the person is injured. You can either use this spell on someone else or yourself. The latter depends on how well you can focus on the spell and yourself. The supplies you need to perform this spell are:

- Myrrh oil

- Three candles (blue, white and purple)

- Sandalwood oil

- Mint oil

- Three pieces of paper

- Three pieces of quartz

Smear or rub the candles with the three oils mentioned above and set them in the shape of a triangle. You need to ensure they form an equal triangle when you place them on the altar. Smear or rub the quartz stone with the oils and place one stone in front of each candle. Now, write the name of the person whom you want to heal on the piece of paper and place it in the center of the triangle. Light the candles, and while you do that, focus on the person you want to heal. Think about their health and how they would be if they were free of the symptoms. Picture their healthy self in your mind while you watch the candles burn. Now, repeat the following three times:

"Magic repair and candles burn,

Illness farewell and health come."

Let the candle burn for exactly three hours before you snuff or blow them out. The person you wanted to heal will soon show some improvement. If you want to add more power to the spell, you cast, perform this ritual three nights in a row.

The Healing Charm

Another simple spell, this has been used for thousands and thousands of years. It was used by ancient occultists as a spell to heal people who were physically ill. Casting this spell requires that you write "Abracadabra" on a sheet of paper. Then, underneath, write the word again but with one letter less. Continue until you have just the one letter left, like this:

ABRACADABRA

ABRACADABR

ABRACADAB

ABRACADA

ABRACAD

ABRACA

ABRAC

ABRA

ABR

AB

A

Roll up the piece of paper as small as you can and place it in a pendant or small vial; wear it on a chain around your neck, and the belief is that the disease symptoms will gradually disappear in the same way as the letters in the word did.

Candle Spells

Spells to Reunite Lovers

These spells are designed to help you rekindle the spark, to bring romance back into your relationship. Many witches choose these spells when they are separated from their loved ones because of work, school, meetings, and other circumstances. However, they can also be used to bring lovers back together after a relationship has broken up. There are other spells you can use in these circumstances as well, and we saw some of those in another part of the book.

Candle Melding Love Spell

When the candles begin to melt, and the wax melds together, you and your partner will be drawn to one another once more.

You will need

- 2 red candles that are shaped like humans
- Some ginger oil

If you can't find any red candles shaped as figures, just use standard candles, so long as they are red. Smear the ginger oil over both candles and then place them in a dish together. They must be in the same dish, not in separate ones, as the candles have to be touching.

Light both candles and focus on positive thoughts of your partner as the wax begins melting. Let the wax from the candles run into each other and focus on the spell and your partner until the candles are sufficiently melted to join together. Repeat the following words until you feel you have got your message across to the universe.

"Candles burn, and wax will run

You and I again are one."

Leave the candles to burn out by themselves.

Return to Me Candle Spell

This is another powerful spell that can help you and your partner reunite. You will need

- Some red yarn or string
- Some vanilla oil
- One candle, either red, white, or pink

Inscribe the candle with your initials or your full name using a sharp implement. Above yours, in the center of the candle, inscribe your partner's name or initials, ensuring you write over the top of the first letters.

Smear oil on the candle and then tie the red yarn around it. Tie it in a bow, making sure the knot is above the initials. Light it and leave it to burn until the flame is getting close to the top carving. Extinguish the candle and leave it near to your altar, letting the universe know that your spell will be completed when your partner has returned to you. Every day, rub more oil over the initials, only stopping when you are reunited.

Flames of Progress

This is a spell designed to help you progress in whatever you want to move forward in, particularly if you find yourself at a sticking point along the road of your life. You may be facing issues such as relationship problems or money worries, and if you can't seem to find a way forward or you've simply lost the motivation to get on, this spell can help you. It can help to give you the motivation you need to help you make improvements in whatever you use the spell for.

You will need

- 3 candles – one white, one dark blue, and one pale blue
- A sharp implement – knife, pin, pen, etc.
- A cinnamon incense stick

Before you start, take the candles, and carve these runes into them:

- Around the center of the white candle, carve the Thurisaz rune
- Around the center of the pale blue candle, carve the Raidho rune
- Around the center of the dark blue candle, carve the Jera rune.

Now put each candle into a holder of its own and place the white candle to the left of you, the dark blue to the right, and the pale blue once in the center.

Take hold of your cinnamon incense stick and focus your attention on whatever issues are troubling you. The incense should be held in your dominant hand. Light it and then, using the flame from the incense, light the white candle.

Extinguish the incense and put it into another holder. Say these words aloud:

"With this flame, the spell is lit.

 I need to move, not to sit."

Light the pale blue candle in the center with the flame from the white candle and say these words:

"With this flame, the spell goes on.

As of now, the delay is gone."

Lastly, use the pale blue candle to light the dark blue candle and say these words to finish the spell:

"With this flame, the spell is cast.

Things will start to move at last."

Look at each of the candles in turn and say the words again in the same order The candles should remain on your altar and be left to go out by themselves, and you should soon start to see things changing in your life.

The Light of Three

This is sometimes used as a kind of dream spell. If you have questions you need answering, it can bring you those answers in the form of a dream.

You will need

- A piece of amethyst or a whole amethyst crystal
- A candle with three wicks
- A jar
- Some sandalwood oil
- Some dried mugwort

Three-wick candles are readily available in any home décor stores, even though they are not a common household candle. Lavender is the best color if you can get it; if not, go for a white one.

Focus your attention on the question you want to be answered and keep it focused throughout the whole spell.

Sprinkle a little dried Mugwort on the surface of the candle. Rub some sandalwood oil over the amethyst. Touch the crystal three times to your forehead, forming a triangular shape as you do. Focus and ask the universe to assist you in opening your third eye.

Now put the crystal onto the candle, positioned in the center of the three wicks. Hold your palm over the top of the candle and voice your question aloud. Light all three wicks and ask the question once more. Leave the candle to burn out by itself, and then, over the next few days, note what you experience in your dreams. If a symbol or a pattern stands out or recurs, that is the answer you are seeking.

Healing Friendships and Relationships

Lots of people think about love spells, about casting spells to make a person fall for them or to stop doing something they should not be doing. There are much better ways that you can achieve this. It isn't always about control and, when things start to get tough, you don't need to be in control of another person – that can often make things much worse. Ask yourself a question – do you have control over the way you respond to a situation? If not, how can you take control? Before you respond to anything, take a bit of time to reflect and ask these questions:

- Is having control over someone unhealthy? Unethical? Is control the only way to deal with a situation?
- If the person involved could understand that their actions affected you, and how, do you think their behavior would be any different?
- If you could understand why the person behaved in that way, could you more easily accept what they have done? Perhaps try to help them?
- Think about your actions – do they have an effect on how that person behaves?

When it comes to healing, to building bridges in friendships or relationships, control is never the answer; instead, you should be looking for a way to see that person in a different light. There's an old saying, "It takes two to tango," and this is very true. It means that both of you should take responsibility for the argument or the upset in your relationship, and it's down to both of you to try to make peace.

To do that, a spell is required, a spell that will help them to see that you are not their enemy. A spell to help bring about better understanding and more love. While you can make a change to how you respond to a person, you can only do it effectively if you understand why they are acting as they are.

For the spell, you will need

- A light blue candle
- Some dried sage
- Some dried catnip
- Some jasmine oil

Take a piece of paper and write down the name of the person. Add a + symbol and then write your own name. Rub the jasmine oil over the candle and then sprinkle dried catnip and dried sage over it. Light the candle, saying the following words as you do so:

"I cannot force you to behave,

A good friendship [or relationship] is what I crave,

A unity of peace and mutual respect,

A showing of love in every aspect.

I call to the unending wisdom of Danu,

To give me insight on just how to reach you,

To question my motives, and search for the good,

To look beyond flaws, so you feel understood,

To open your eyes too, so you understand,

That a love worth having is worth fighting for,

That you cherish those that love you and love them back more."

Light the candle and burn it every night before bed, just for a few minutes. Always remember to put the candle out before you go to sleep – do not blow it out as you can upset the elements; instead, snuff it out.

Reuniting The Reflections Spell

The reuniting spell uses a mirror, divining the power from it to help you and a loved one reunite.

You will need

- Some paper made from fine linen
- A pen
- A mirror
- A piece of each of the following crystals – red jasper, rose quartz, garnet, and carnelian

Write down your name on the linen paper, making sure to write your full name – no nicknames! Underneath your name, write down the name of the person you want to reunite with.

Place the paper, so it is facing the mirror glass and is reflected in it. Move the mirror slightly, just so that it is facing but not resting on the paper. The best type of mirror is a makeup mirror that has a tilting stand.

Scatter the crystals over your names on the paper and say these words several times:

"Mirror, mirror, do you see?

Bring my lover back to me."

Soon, you will hear that the person you miss so much is coming back.

You must keep in mind that this spell can only work if the person you want to reunite with has loved you at some point or still does.

If you are trying to force a person to fall for you, then you are wandering into the realms of black magic, because you are attempting to take control of their emotions. That is not Wicca; that isn't what it's all about.

Safe Revenge Spell

Sometimes, if someone has caused you hurt, you want them to know how much they have hurt you; you want them to understand how their actions have affected you. This doesn't give you permission to dive into using black magic, not at all. There are some safe spells that you can use to help that person understand the effect they had on you.

First, focus on the person who caused you the hurt. Make a mental list of all their shortcomings. Next, consider their higher being and mentally list all the reasons they struggle to live up to that being – how they struggle and why.

Think about a positive quality that you would like this person to have. You do this, so your spell doesn't cause their lives any damage. Let's say, for example, that you want payback for a drug dealer, perhaps because you know he sells to young people, or he forces people to do his dealing for him. That positive quality could be a conscience. That might make it hard for them to sell their drugs in the future because, all of a sudden, that conscience kicks in and stops them. You could also request that the universe opens their heart, so they can see the people around them, understand them and even, maybe, love them.

When you ask for a positive quality from the universe, choose from these:

- Clarity

- Connection to a higher source of spirituality

- Enlightenment

- Freedom

- Honor
- Intelligence
- Love
- Opening the heart and the soul
- Understanding
- Vision

All of these qualities will affect the way the recipient behaves. The badness that surrounds their identity will break apart, and they begin to hurt, to suffer as they have made others suffer. If any one of these qualities came back at you threefold, think of how much you would gain! You would gain in these three primary ways:

- You get to take revenge on a person who has ignored his higher calling and not lived up to his higher being
- When it comes to their higher being, you get to do the right thing
- As a bonus, what you send out to the universe, you get back, In other words, you reap what you sow

To do this spell:

Light a candle (any candle) and sit before it. Call on the person you are focused on and then call on his higher being. Ask his higher being what the best quality would be to ask for so that you can be instrumental in bringing about change in their lives.

Say the positive quality out loud and read these words:

"Upon the planes in which I live,

The gift of [insert quality] I now give,

To [insert the name of the revenge target] with all my heart and soul,

To change [him/her] and to make [him/her] whole;

By all on high and law of three,

This is my will, so shall it be."

Visualize that person in the flames of the candle, just for a few minutes, and then extinguish the candle. You have completed the spell, and now, you can sit back and wait for it to take effect.

Find a New Job

Either write your own job advertisement or find the job you want to apply for. For this spell to work, you must create an ideal situation for yourself and visualize it. Therefore, you must be specific about the location, job, and salary. You can also add more details to your visualization if needed since the effect of the spell is greater when you add more details; however, you should be realistic. Do not expect too much of the Universe. For this spell, you need to light a large deep blue candle. Blue represents the planet Jupiter, and most witches perform rituals to worship Jupiter when they need jobs. Place the lit candle on a metal tray.

Now, read the advertisement you created or read numerous times and fold the paper into a cone. Burn the paper over the flame and let the ash from the paper fall into the tray. Once the paper is fully burned, collect the ashes and place them in a bag or box. If the candle goes out, do not worry too much. Light the candle again. Let the Universe know you are persistent and want to get the job.

Bury the bag or box with the ashes under an oak, ash, or another energy tree close to the place you want to work. If there is no such tree around the area, bury the ashes in a flowerpot, preferably one with a peppermint plant since peppermint is an energizer. This is when your ritual comes to an end. The most important part of this spell is to get a job, so you cannot forget this step.

Now, end the magic spell. You will see the results in some time, but this does not mean you stop looking for a job. Always be attentive and grab opportunities that work for you.

Find Your Dream Job

You should cast this spell only after you send the application or resume to the employer. Use a sharp knife or [in to write the name of the company where you want to work on a large green candle. Take a red candle and carve the victory rune, also known as Tiwaz. This rune looks like an upward pointing arrow. Write your full name under the rune.

Burn these candles for 30 minutes after the sunsets on Thursday, and visualize yourself getting the job you so badly want. After 30 minutes, snuff the candle out. Do not blow out the candles. Wet your fingers and put out the candles. Now, use the same candles every Thursday and watch them burn for 15 minutes while you visualize yourself getting the job. Do this until the candles until you get a job, or they are fully extinguished. Throw the candles away and leave a small bowl of milk at night after you get the job. This is a way to say thanks.

Chapter Eleven: Crystals and Magic

When you perform any magic, using crystal energy, you need to ensure you choose the right crystals for yourself. To do this, you must use your intuition to help you identify the right crystal for you. Crystals are often used in Wicca to direct energy towards different objects. They can also be used to store energy collected during a ritual or spell for safekeeping. Therefore, it is important that you choose the right crystal when you perform any ritual or cast a spell using a crystal.

Crystals have a special ability to store or emit energy, and every crystal has a different vibration or frequency. You can use the energy in the crystals to help you overcome various issues in life. You can also increase the intensity of the spells you cast using crystals. The crystals are better than regular rocks, and all have a geometric pattern, which is the reason behind the energy in the crystals. These geometric patterns are more intricate than the cell structure in the human body. Before we look at different methods to choose a crystal, let us look at some crystal types.

Types

Clear Quartz

This is the best crystal to use for healing. This has no negative effects whatsoever but needs to be cleansed before you use it. You can use the energy in this crystal to clear different types of energies in your body – physical, mental, spiritual, and emotional. You can align the energy in the chakras and your aura. This crystal can be cleaned easily.

You will find it very easy to program the crystal, which will help you balance all the energies in your body. You can create a great impression on your soul.

Onyx

This crystal helps to balance opposing forces of energy – the yin and the yang. You can reduce any form of stress in your body when you use this crystal. You can exercise a good level of self-control and will find happiness in the smallest things. Good fortune becomes your very good friend.

Opal

The opal crystal is a brilliant one since it works on improving all your attributes. You can enhance your creativity and imagination. A student would love this crystal since he or she would be able to improve his memory, which would prove beneficial for them during the examinations. It also helps to remove any inhibitions you may have.

Moonstone

This is a crystal that is often used by women since it always keeps them calm during pregnancy and the menstrual cycle. The energy is always balanced, and so are the thoughts in mind. It is because of this crystal that clairvoyants find their capabilities increasing and sharpening. You can balance certain areas in your body using this crystal. You can keep any negative emotions at bay. The moonstone crystal helps to stimulate confidence in you and will balance all your feelings and emotions. You can perceive things around you much better than you ever had. A woman will benefit from using this crystal since it enhances the feminine nature.

Rose Quartz

This crystal is one that depicts every aspect of love. You can use this crystal to cast various love spells. This crystal helps you understand your desires and emotions better and can understand all your feelings. You can increase your trust and faith in the people around you. You can love yourself unconditionally, which will help to introduce you to your inner self. You can remove any depression and grief. The love that you have for yourself will help you overcome any negative thoughts you may have about yourself. Any resentment that you feel towards the people around you will vanish when you use this crystal. The best combination of this crystal is amethyst.

Moss Agate

It is also known as Dendritic Agate or tree Agate. It is a semi-opaque stone with wisps of white and green that resembles Moss and hence its name. These stones are used for their protective and healing abilities. Moss Agate is believed to help strengthen one's connection with the elements- earth.

Red Goldstone

It is also known as red sandstone, and it is essentially a bright orange-red colored gem with specks of gold. It is associated with the sacred chakra and promotes creativity, drive, and confidence in the wearer. Red sandstone is formed when copper salts are added to molten glass.

Rudraksha Seeds

Rudraksha is not a crystal or a stone, but it is worth learning more about this seed. A rudraksha seed is believed to have miraculous powers. This seed is important in Hinduism, and numerous scriptures, including the Vedas, talk about how these seeds benefit the human race. According to Hindu mythology, these seeds were created from the tears shed by Lord Shiva. You can wear a seed around your neck if you think someone is using black magic against you.

Turquoise

Turquoise is a blue-green stone that is beautiful to look at. This stone has many healing properties, and it is believed that it is a key to the door between earth and heaven. The energy in this stone will help you connect with the energy in the universe. Many Native American tribes believe that this stone helps people reach enlightenment. Chinese healers also use this stone in their native healing rituals. This stone is associated with the throat chakra. If there are any imbalances in the throat chakra, they can be removed using this stone.

Prehnite

This stone is yellow-green in color and can be either translucent or opaque. It contains little specks of black rutile present in it. It is quite popular among healers and wisdom seekers. It is believed that this stone gives the strength that's necessary for facing the realities of life with grace and patience. This stone is also associated with the heart chakra and helps remove any negative energy, which is stagnant and one's body because of any old injuries or grievances. Empaths often use it because it can heal the healers. This stone helps strengthen one's feelings of empathy.

Choosing the Right Crystal

Now that you are aware of the different crystals and also their significance, you must learn how to select the right crystals for you. Remember that different crystals have different effects on your body, and the crystals that work for another person may not necessarily work for you. You can choose the crystals for yourself based on the trial and error method. This section will discuss different techniques you can use to determine which crystal is right for you.

Call Upon the Crystal

When you choose a crystal for yourself, call upon the energies in the universe to assess whether a specific crystal will work for you or not. You can ask the universe to send you signs and help you choose the right crystals for you. When you do this, you can choose the right crystals since you know the Universe will not lead you astray. You should remember to keep an open mind and receive the energy from the crystal.

Physical Reaction

Every crystal has a specific energy, and one of the easiest ways to determine if a crystal is right for you or not is to place your non-dominant hand over the crystal. If the energy in the crystal calls towards your hand, then this is the right crystal for you. You can use this crystal to perform different spells. If you want to select healing stones, hold the crystal in your hand, and feel the energy within the crystal. Pay attention to how your body reacts to the energy in the crystal. Close your eyes, and pay attention to the sensation in your hand. Start working with your non-dominant hand and then move the crystal to your dominant hand.

Different Properties

If you know that there are specific wants that you want to address using a crystal, make a list of those wants. When you have the list, make a list of the crystals that will help you fulfill those needs. One of the best ways to do this is to look for a crystal that will heal a chakra or a specific part of your body. As mentioned earlier, there are seven chakras in the body, and each of these chakras is associated with different colors. For example, if you want to heal the root chakra, you should look for a red-colored crystal. Read through the sections above to associate a color with each chakra in your body. Different crystals are also associated with different elements. If you want to work with a specific element, you should use the crystal associated with that element.

Cleansing and Clearing

You should clean the crystals well if you want to maintain the energy within the crystals. So, make sure you cleanse the crystals, especially if you use them frequently or have not used them in a while. Cleanse the crystals when you purchase them and also every few days after you use them. Since crystals store energy, they may also absorb some negative energy during a spell. This will only damage the crystal and render it useless to you. One of the easiest ways to cleanse a crystal is to place it either in moonlight or sunlight. You should let the natural light course through your crystal and clean the energy within the crystal.

Research

Understand the different types of crystals you can use to cast various spells and perform rituals. Purchase a crystal only when you know and understand its properties.

Purpose

It is also important to know why you want to use a specific crystal. It is only when you understand that you can choose the right crystal. You will need to choose small stones if you want to use a crystal in jewelry. If you want to use them during meditation, you should use medium-sized crystals. You can use large crystals if you want to use them to cleanse other crystals you are using. Keep the following questions in mind when you want to identify the purpose:

1. How do you want to use the crystals?

2. Where do you want to place the crystals?

3. What spells do you want to cast using the crystals?

4. Do you want only to cast love spells?

When you answer these questions, you will know which crystal you want to purchase for yourself.

Rituals

Motivational Ritual

If you need Monday motivation and find it hard to get out of bed to get to work, why not try the quick motivation ritual? You can get your work done like a boss when you perform this ritual. To perform this ritual, you need red jasper. This crystal is grounded and is the perfect stone to help you get down to business. The stone's energy encourages you and supports you.

Hold the crystal in the palm of your dominant hand, and focus on the energy in the crystal. Now, let the energy in the crystal guide you towards the areas you need to improve. When you hold onto the stone, ask yourself what areas in your life you need to take action in, and listen to the stone tell you what you must do.

Creativity Ritual

Since creativity benefits people in every area of life, regardless of whether it is a relationship, art practice, work, or even your picture grid on Instagram, it is important to let the creative juices flow. You can use the energy from different crystals to open your creative channel and let yourself feel more inspired and original. To perform this ritual, you must use a carnelian. This crystal is a powerful stone and calls the creative energy situated in your sacral chakra.

Hold the crystal in the palm of your dominant hand, and say the following words aloud, "I am creative." These words hold immense power, and their intent is enhanced by the energy in the crystal.

Chapter Twelve: Wicca Herbal Magic

Since the plant kingdom developed on Earth well before human beings evolved, you can say that herbs are one of the oldest magical objects or tools that exist. Plants have many properties that help people maintain both spiritual and physical wellbeing. When healers, medicine men, and shamans incorporated different species of plants into their practices, herbal magic began to gain popularity. Before magic was separated from medicine, people used to accompany physical healing with prayer and ritual. They used an herbal tea or concoction and performed a ritual or repeated an incantation for a speedy recovery. People now know that a cup of herbal tea has both spiritual and emotional effects and also has nutritional effects and benefits for people. Since herbs are used for their magical healing properties, people who cast spells must learn more about herbal magic, and learn about the different herbs they can use when they cast spells.

Elemental Power of Plants

When it comes to the various symbols used in magic, plants embody or signify the power of the four elements working together. Since plants begin as seeds in the soil, they need minerals and vitamins to sustain. They also interact with sunlight, which acts as a catalyst to convert carbon dioxide into oxygen. This directly affects the air quality around the plant. The air around the plant can foster more life in the environment through the wind. Wind stimulates the growth of leaves and stems. It also scatters seeds between plants to continue the cycle of growth. Since plants also need some water to live, they play a crucial role in the regulation of the water cycle. They help to purify water and move it from the soil into the atmosphere. It is for this reason; spell casters use plants or herbs to enhance the strength of the energy used during a ritual. Plants represent how the four elements work together.

Plant Intelligence

The famous Greek philosopher, Aristotle, believed that even plants have psyches, and many witches or Wiccans believe the same. Psyche is a word used to describe the human spirit or soul. Scientists also have found evidence to prove that plants do have a certain level of consciousness. Research shows that plants can feel pain.

It is known that plants communicate and cooperate with various beings in the wild and with other plants. They also cooperate with different plant species. Consider a forest setting. In this setting, every shrub, tree and plant exchanges information with each other using an underground network of fungi and roads. This network allows various plants to exchange minerals and vitamins with each other and help each other by making up for any shortages during the growing phase. This is similar to you borrowing eggs or sugar from a neighbor and returning the favor in the future with a little extra butter or cake. For instance, if an insect bites a flower or leaf, the plant releases various chemicals to repel the insect. These chemicals act as a stimulus and prompt the neighboring plants to release the chemicals to repel the same insects.

These discoveries help people understand a plant's intelligence. Regardless of whether you work with the plant seeds, roots, leaves, stems, berries, or flowers, you can tap into this magical energy when you use herbs in your practice.

Versatile and Hand-On Magic

It is good to work with plants or herbs from your own magical garden, especially if you want to connect with the energies present in the earth. When you harvest and grow herbs in your garden, you are in touch with various energies in the Earth, including rain, wind, sun, and the energy of the various insects and animal life. What is more is that when you garden, you can charge various tools you use with your energy. You also transfer some of your energy into the soil, which means your energy is used as part of the various life and death cycles taking place in the garden.

Herbs are the most versatile magical objects or tools you can use when you cast spells or perform rituals. You can use herbs to create various magical crafts, such as puppets, spell jars, dream pillows, sachets, and other objects. Some practitioners also create their own oils and incense using herbs, and these add more power to their spell work. Herbs can also be used in the kitchen. You can create magical tinctures, baked goods, potions, teas, and other foods and beverages using herbs. Most practitioners use herbs in different forms of spell work, right from candle magic to bath spells. Some spells require the caster to smudge the dried herbs or use dried herbs to remove any negative energy before they perform any ritual or cast a spell.

Some practitioners also use specific herbs to mark the protective circle before they begin their Sabbat rituals. There are some who also use specific herbs to honor their deities or natural elements, such as lemon balm or lavender. The former is sacred to Diana, the Roman goddess. Herbal magic is practical, and most of it can be done with various ingredients that you already have in your kitchen.

What is an Herb?

There are various characteristics that separate herbs from other plants in the plant kingdom. For cooks, Witches, and healers, an herb can be anything that is useful to people. They may use herbs for the following purposes:

- Medicine

- To add fragrance

- In cooking

- Clothing

- Spiritual and magical work

Trees and shrubs are also included in the list of herbs. You can also include vegetables, fruit, flowers, grass, and other plants that some cultures or traditions believe are weeds.

It is important to note that for both herbalists and Witches, an herb is a plant that benefits the body. Herbs can also include toxic plants, such as henbane and belladonna. People who understand herbs know that no plant is good or bad. Every plant has its own specific uses, especially when it comes to the human body. If you are only starting with herbal magic, ensure that you follow all warnings about toxic herbs. Listen to what experts have to say about herbs, and remember it is better to be safe than sorry. Always look for non-toxic substitutes when you cast spells.

How to Get Started with Herbal Magic

There is a lot of information available about herbal magic, and it can be overwhelming when you first read about it. You, however, do not have to be a master at botany or a gardener to begin your practice. All you must do is to acquaint yourself with some of the herbs. One of the best ways to build a relationship with the energy in the plant world is to spend some time with the herbs.

Most herbs used in magic can be found in the spice section at the supermarket. If you are starting out with Wicca, try some simple herbal spells and begin casting complex ones as you gradually build your knowledge.

Conclusion

Wicca is a practice of witchcraft and spell work, and there are only a few who completely understand what this tradition or practice is. Most people worry that this practice is based on lies since there are quite a few people out there who do not believe in magic or witchcraft.

Wicca is traditionally practiced in Western culture, and the practitioners use energy from the natural elements and other beings to perform their rituals or cast spells. The Wiccan tradition is based on the principle of never causing harm to another individual. That said, it is hard to determine what harm is since it is a relative concept, but Wiccans must never willfully harm another being, especially when they cast a spell.

Most spells in the Wiccan tradition are based on white magic, and this magic is pure and does not cause harm to another being. There are other forms of magic, namely red and black magic, that are considered evil, and only some witches perform such magic. This book sheds some light on the different forms of magic to help understand more about Wicca. Since Wicca is based on white magic, any spell you cast does not affect another individual.

Most people avoided discussing Wicca and Witchcraft until the early 1950s when Gerald Gardner began to talk about magic and witchcraft. He had also set up a coven, known as the Bricket Wood Coven, and was the High Priest. Soon Doreen Valiente joined Gardner as the High Priestess, and the two of them rewrote the Book of Shadows. This book had all the information a Witch needed about the craft and also some common practices that Wiccans need to adhere to.

If you are new to the practice of Wicca, you may have many questions about tradition and culture. This book provides all the information you need about the practice. The book starts off by explaining what Wicca is, and the various aspects of Wicca. It also talks about how Wicca has obtained some traditions and cultures from occult practices. The book also sheds some light on how Gerald Gardner, known as the Father of Wicca, used some principles of Occult to set the framework for Wicca.

The book also tells you about the different methods you need to follow when you cast your first spell or perform your ritual. If you are a novice, you must first learn various tips and tricks to help you cast spells successfully. Since you use your energy and energy from other sources, such as the objects placed on the altar, you need to ensure you create a protective circle around yourself to prevent the influence of any negative energy. The book also tells you what you must do to create a protective circle around you, and how you should come out of the circle after you perform a ritual or cast a spell.

As mentioned earlier, Wiccan practitioners use white magic to cast their spells since they do not want to harm anybody. There are, however, other forms of magic known as red and black magic. These forms of magic are considered dark or negative forms of magic since the objective is the harm another individual or use their energy force to cast the spell. A ritual or practice of Wicca known as sex magic is also considered red magic, but this depends on your intentions. If you cast a spell using sex magic with the permission of your partner, then you are not causing anybody harm. Both of you are working towards the same intent, giving a stronger chance of that intent manifesting itself in the world.

Any form of magic is only as strong as the spell caster's intent, and if you want to cast the right spells and manifest your intent in the world, use the energy within yourself and in the objects in your altar to intensity the intent. This book also leaves you with different spells you can use to attract love, money, and prosperity. It also sheds some light on different protection and healing spells you can use to safeguard yourself, your home, and the people you love.

Since Wicca allows the use of different objects, people tend to use crystals and herbs to intensify or enhance their intent. They also use these objects to perform rituals and spells. This book also provides information on herbal magic and crystal magic. You learn how to choose the right crystal and also perform simple rituals to improve your creativity.

If you are a novice, you can use this book as your guide. It has all the information you need about Wicca and helps you cast the right spells. It will teach you the different traditions and rules you must follow when you cast spells or perform any ritual.

Resources

https://Wiccanow.com/home-protection-spell/

https://wiccaliving.com/law-of-attraction/

HTTPS://SAMANTHAMARSWRITER.BLOGSPOT.COM/2013/01/PROTECTION-SPELL.HTML

https://www.free-witchcraft-spells.com/wellbeing-spells.html

https://www.free-witchcraft-spells.com/weight-loss-spells.html

https://www.free-witchcraft-spells.com/energy-spells.html

https://www.free-witchcraft-spells.com/happiness-spells.html

https://hubpages.com/religion-philosophy/Top-5-Money-Attraction-Rituals

https://wiccaliving.com/wheel-of-the-year-Wiccan-sabbats/

https://www.wikihow.com/Do-White-Magic

https://www.womenofgrace.com/blog/?p=55059

https://isha.sadhguru.org/in/en/wisdom/article/black-magic

https://witchcraftway.com/spells/love-spells/a-red-candle-love-spell/

HTTPS://WWW.COSMOPOLITAN.COM/SEX-LOVE/A31994289/HOW-TO-DO-A-LOVE-SPELL/

https://www.allure.com/story/how-to-cast-love-spells

HTTPS://WWW.LLEWELLYN.COM/SPELL.PHP?SPELL_ID=7022 HTTPS://MOODYMOONS.COM/2019/08/12/LOVE-GODDESS-SPELL-POPPET-TUTORIAL/

https://www.free-witchcraft-spells.com/healing-spells.html

https://www.free-witchcraft-spells.com/free-easy-love-spells.html

https://www.free-witchcraft-spells.com/white-magic-love-spells.html

https://www.free-witchcraft-spells.com/free-money-spells.html

https://www.free-witchcraft-spells.com/free-spells-for-money.html

https://www.free-witchcraft-spells.com/candle-spells.html

https://www.free-witchcraft-spells.com/reunite-lovers-spells.html

https://www.free-witchcraft-spells.com/free-candle-spells.html

https://www.free-witchcraft-spells.com/easy-magic-spells.html

HTTPS://WWW.WATTPAD.COM/594502699-WICCAN-WITCHCRAFT-SPELLS-AND-INFORMATION

https://wiccaliving.com/beginners-guide-herbal-magic/

https://magic-spells-and-potions.com/safe_revenge_spell.html

https://lovemagicworks.com/get-job/

www.ingramcontent.com/pod-product-compliance
Lightning Source LLC
Chambersburg PA
CBHW071618080526
44588CB00010B/1172